CHRISTMAS WITH GOD

Quiet Moments with God

RACINE, WI

For to us a child is born,
to us a son is given,
and the government will be on his shoulders.
And he will be called Wonderful Counselor,
Mighty God,
Everlasting Father,
Prince of Peace.

ISAIAH 9:6

Christmas with God

ISBN: 978-1-970103-84-7 - *Paperback*
ISBN: 978-1-970103-85-4 - *Hardcover*
ISBN: 978-1-970103-46-5 - *Ebook*

Copyright © 2022 by Honor Books
Racine, WI

Manuscript written and compiled by Rebecca Barlow Jordan, Sarah M. Hupp, Fran Caffey Sandin, Robert Exley, Linda Gilden, and Sue Rhodes Dodd.

Cover Design by Faille Schmitz.

The Reason for the Season

To us a child is born.
ISAIAH 9:6

Sleigh bells ring,
Are you listening?
In the lane,
Snow is glistening!
A beautiful sight,
We're happy tonight
Walkin' in a winter wonderland!
DICK SMITH AND FELIX BERNARD

It's Christmas! The season for giving, for loving, for celebrating. All around us are joyous reminders of this happy season. Twinkling Christmas lights. Holiday music on the radio. Promises of snow on the evening weather forecast. The smell of fresh pine. Just-baked gingerbread cookies.

And all around us are stressful reminders, too: Irritated shoppers and crowded malls. Honking horns and traffic snarls. Frantic meal preparations and credit card debt. Sometimes we get so caught up in the seasonal madness that we forget why we even celebrate Christmas at all.

But it doesn't have to be that way. Don't forget the true reason for the season: Love. God's love. And His love pierces this world's darkness.

One of the traditions of Christmas is the celebration of Advent, a heart preparation for the coming Savior. If we are willing to save money for Christmas gifts, to make a mailing list for Christmas cards, to shop for weeks, and to schedule holiday get-togethers, surely we can make time to prepare our hearts for the coming of our Emmanuel.

O come, Thou Dayspring,
come and cheer
Our spirits by thine advent here
And drive away the shades of night
And pierce the clouds and bring us light
Rejoice! Rejoice! Emmanuel
Shall come to thee O Israel!
ISAAC WATTS

Spend a quiet moment with God. Read. Pray. Reflect. Savor memories—old and new. Focus on the love and laughter that make Christmas so special. Prepare your heart for His coming.

This year, spend *Christmas with God*—you won't regret it!

Nothing but Socks

Do not be afraid; I will provide for you.
G E N E S I S   5 0 : 2 1   N A S B

Christmas was only a few days away, but a long-distance move and mounting bills meant that gifts were out of the question. The couple agreed to give one another their love for Christmas, but knowing that there wouldn't be a small gift for her husband saddened the young wife. "Oh, Lord," she sighed, "Isn't there something You can do?"

As she reached to hang up her coat, a few coins jingled in the pocket. When she turned the pocket inside out, she found only fifty cents. *Fifty cents wouldn't buy much of a present, but at least it would be something,* she reasoned.

The young woman walked a few blocks to the local market, glancing at the shopping cart beside the door that held merchandise for sale at reduced prices. Today the cart was overflowing with socks. The store was discontinuing all clothing to make room for snack items, so the manager had marked the socks down to ten cents per two-pair package! Overjoyed, the young wife snatched up five of the precious bundles. If she wrapped each sock individually, her husband would have twenty packages to unwrap on Christmas!

But on Christmas morning, there were *forty* packages under the Christmas tree. Twenty of them were for her! As the young couple began to unwrap their packages, they began to laugh. Every package under the tree contained nothing but socks! Her husband had also found the shopping cart of socks and had spent fifty cents on her! God had answered her prayer and provided both with a warm memory and warm feet that Christmas!

Sometimes Miracles Hide

I am greatly encouraged; in all our troubles my
joy knows no bounds.
2 CORINTHIANS 7:4

Charles Dickens' book *A Christmas Carol* has become one of the best-loved stories of all time. But few know that it grew out of one of the darkest periods in the author's career and changed his life forever.

At age thirty-one and at the peak of his career, Dickens was facing serious financial trouble. Unexpected news that his other novels were not selling well stunned the young man and resurfaced memories and insecurities of his childhood poverty. He supported a large extended family, and his wife was expecting their fifth child. What would he do?

After months of depression, Dickens was walking through the black streets of London where "bawdy streetwalkers, pickpockets, footpads, and beggars" roamed. The scene reminded him of a recurring nightmare: a twelve-year-old boy working "twelve hours a day, six days a week, attaching labels on the endless stream of pots to earn the six shillings that will keep him alive." Sitting in that dingy, rat-infested warehouse, the boy saw that the light outside was fading, along with his hopes. His father was in debtors' prison, and the boy felt helpless, abandoned.

The dream was a true scene from Dickens' childhood. Fortunately, his father inherited some money, paid his debts, and was released from prison.

Suddenly, Dickens knew he must write A *Christmas Carol* for those people he saw who could identify with his own fears. Strangely, with Scrooge's change of heart in the novel and Dickens' festive description of Christmas cheer and celebrations, Dickens' own depression laded. The much-loved book helped restore his confidence and paved the way to many more treasured stories.[1]

Like Dickens' experience, miracles often hide in the midst of self-doubt and confusion. Focusing on the joys of Christmas renews our hope in the season and restores our faith in what God can accomplish through us.

———————————————————

Harmonious Discord

*Finally, all of you, live in harmony with one
another; be sympathetic, love as brothers, be
compassionate and humble.*

1 PETER 3:8

Squeak, squeal, honk, jingle, squeak, ping! The cousins' Christmas Eve orchestra played its first number. Since there hadn't been an official practice until moments before the performance, the young musicians were still working to perfect their presentation.

Several weeks before Christmas, Aunt Jo had sent music to each cousin according to his or her instrument. The orchestra consisted of one viola, two trumpets, a French horn, a triangle, a xylophone, a snare drum, conga drums, and a piano.

Despite occasional discord, the Christmas carols were recognizable, each selection punctuated by giggles and occasional laughter.

"David, you can't rest *now.* Pick up your trumpet!"

"Celia, get ready, your note is next!"

"Hanes, jump back in on the next measure. We need you."

The adults sang along and smiled at this delightful new family tradition. The resident eleven-year-old dramatist introduced each song with Scripture, adding meaning to the melodies.

Three distinctly different families, all blood-related yet living in different towns, came together for this moment and were connected by something special. Maybe it was the Christmas spirit. Maybe it was the family spirit. Maybe it was the Holy Spirit. Maybe it was all three.

It is not necessary for us all to play the same instrument, have the same interests, nor enjoy the same sports. But we can be in harmony, simply by our shared heritage as children of God.

––––––––––––––––––––

A Birthday Party for Jesus

For today in the city of David there has been born for you a Savior, who is Christ the Lord.
LUKE 2:11 NASB

How would you feel if you had a birthday party and the people attending gave presents to one another but not to you?

That's the question Mable Dumas addressed at her prayer group's holiday party. As the ladies arrived in her home, she served refreshments and then said, "Ladies, we like to visit with one another, but from this point on, let's talk only about Jesus. He is our guest of honor, and it's His birthday."

As the women gathered around the fireplace, Mable sat on the hearth and led a conversation about Jesus. The focal point became a wooden nativity set.

The ladies discussed everything from Gabriel's visit to Mary to the astonishing moment when God became so small for our sakes—our Savior, lying on a clump of hay.

Then Mable announced, "Every birthday party has gifts. Now it's time for us to give our gifts to Jesus." She passed around a basket filled with tiny, decorated boxes. At the appointed time, each participant opened her box in an attitude of prayer and read aloud a Scripture, along with the companion "gift" to place on an altar. These included such things as:

- *My heart*
- *My faith*
- *My future*
- *My dreams*

During the touching, intimate moment, several women moved to a kneeling position and then wept softly. That day became special, because the ladies chose to give Jesus the most meaningful gift of all: *themselves.*

Toy Boxes and Heart Gifts

*Inasmuch as ye have done it unto one of the least
of these my brethren, ye have done it unto me.*
MATTHEW 25:40 KJV

Twenty large toy boxes lined the front of the auditorium — brightly painted and beautifully decorated. The lids were open with the names of children visible on the inside of each. As families came into the building, parents came forward with their children and placed gifts in the appropriate toy box. It wasn't long until every single toy box was filled to the brim.

The pastor stepped forward and began the morning service. The highlight of the service, though, was not the sermon; it was the choir from the Children's Home — yes, the very same children for whom the toy boxes were filled. They sang with transparent gratitude to the Father and an overpowering love for the Savior. This was their Christmas, and the small church in Austin, Texas, was their family.

Later that evening, Heather looked up at her father and asked, "Dad, do those kids really not have a mom or dad?"

"Yes, that's true," he replied.

"Well, then I feel good that we gave them presents, but won't they be sad without a mom and dad?"

"Sweetheart, I am sure that there are days in their lives when they are very sad. But I also know that they are very special to Jesus. And because of people like you and your brother, they know that they are loved."

"That's good!" she replied.

Without a doubt, this was one of the best Christmas gifts that could have ever been given to Heather and her brother Will, for they experienced the joy that comes from loving and giving as Jesus commanded.

———————————————————

Joy from the Inside Out

But the angel said to them, "Do not be afraid.
I bring you good news of great joy that will be
for all the people."
LUKE 2:10

Who hasn't read the famous Dr. Seuss story of *How the Grinch Stole Christmas?* When the wicked Grinch hears all the hoopla of Christmas celebrations in Whoville, he determines to destroy every shred of joy in town. Disguised as Santa he plots carefully, assembles a sleigh, and ties reindeer horns to his dog, Max, for Rudolph. Then as Christmas Eve approaches, the Grinch sweeps into every home, sucking up all the trees, gifts, stockings, and toys left by Santa for every boy and girl.

When little Cindy-Lou-Who catches the Grinch in the act of stealing, the devilish robber thinks up a lame excuse to satisfy the child: He claims the tree lights are in need of repair and he will quickly return the tree in working order.

The Grinch roars through town — up one chimney and down another — until he has stolen every reminder of Christmas in Who-ville. But to his dismay the next morning, the Grinch hears the townspeople of Who-ville laughing and singing. Why would Who-ville be celebrating Christmas without boxes, packages, or ribbons?

The wicked Grinch ultimately concludes that Christmas must mean something more than just traditional toys, gift-giving, and store-bought packages. And you know the rest of the story: The Grinch's heart grows three sizes that day, and he returns every toy, package, ornament, and Christmas tree to the children and families of Who-ville.

The simple truth is: the Grinch learned the real meaning of Christmas, and every year the same challenge arises for each of us.

Would we, too, agree with the people of Who-ville if every good thing was suddenly whisked away from us? Could it be that the joy of Christmas really is found not on the inside of stores, but on the inside of our hearts?

Keep Your Eyes on Him

*Let us fix our eyes on Jesus, the author and
perfecter of our faith, who for the joy set before
him endured the cross, scorning its shame, and
sat down at the right hand of the throne of God.*
HEBREWS 12:2

Ginger ran to her mother's room as fast as her five-year-old legs would take her. "Come look; come quick," she squealed.

"What is it, honey?" her mother asked.

"You have to come see."

Ginger grabbed Mother by the hand and led her to the living room. Stopping in front of the credenza, Ginger pointed her chubby little finger to the manger scene.

When Mother had arranged the figures the previous night, the display was properly balanced and evenly spaced. The larger figures were near the stable, and the smaller ones were at the far edge of the walnut top so as to achieve proper perspective. Mother had been pleased with the visual picture. Now the figures were clustered under the stable roof. Each stood facing the manger, as close as possible to the Baby Jesus.

"Isn't that better? Now they can all see," Ginger proudly exclaimed.

"See?" asked her puzzled mother.

"Yes, see," said Ginger. "When I got up, all the men were scattered around. Some of them were so far away that they couldn't see Baby Jesus. I moved them closer so they could see Him."

Can you see Jesus, or do you need to move a little closer to the manger this season in order to see the Savior?

Someone Who Understands

*Who, being in very nature God . . . made himself
nothing, taking the very nature of a servant,
being made in human likeness.*
PHILIPPIANS 2:6-1

One Christmas Eve a man refused to attend church with his wife. He was a good man but could not believe the Christmas story of God coming to earth as a man. So he stayed at home and waited for his family to return later.

Shortly after, snow began to fall heavily. A loud thud against his front door startled the man. When the sounds continued, he opened the front door to investigate. There he saw a flock of birds, huddled in the snow. In a desperate search for shelter, they had tried to fly through his large front window.

The man felt sorry for the birds and tried to direct them to a barn in the back of his house. He opened the

22

barn doors and turned on a light. But the birds would not come. The man scattered bread crumbs on the snow, making a trail from the front door to the stable entrance. Still the birds ignored him. He tried catching them, and then shooing at them. They only scattered.

Realizing the birds were frightened, he thought, *If only I can think of some way to make them trust me. If only I could be a bird, talk with them, speak their language. Then I could show them the way – so they could really hear and see and understand.*

About that time, the church bells began to ring. As he listened to the glad tidings of Christmas, the truth dawned. The man sank to his knees in the snow.[2]

Just like those little frightened birds could only relate to another bird like themselves, God sent His Son Jesus to earth so that He could relate to us, and we to Him. The next time your friends are hurt or lonely and in need of someone to talk to, let them know that there is someone who truly hears and sees and understands where they are and what they're going through.

That someone is Jesus.

———————————————

A Permanent Companion

And surely I am with you always,
to the very end of the age.
MATTHEW 28:20

What little girl wouldn't love to see a new doll waiting for her under the Christmas tree? One that eats, wets, talks, walks — or one that is nothing but a silent bedtime companion. Every year the toy shelves burst with new models, just waiting to be dubbed the child's favorite doll.

Author Dale Galloway shares a story by R. E. Thomas that makes us rethink just what constitutes a "favorite" among some children:

"Do you like dollies?" the little girl asked her house guest.

"Yes, very much," the man responded.

"Then I'll show you mine," was the reply. Thereupon she presented one by one a whole family of dolls.

"And now tell me," the visitor asked, "which is your favorite doll?"

The child hesitated for a moment and then she said, "You're quite sure you like dollies, and will you please promise not to smile if I show you my favorite?" The man solemnly promised, and the girl hurried from the room. In a moment she returned with a tattered and dilapidated old doll. Its hair had come off; its nose was broken; its cheeks were scratched; an arm and a leg were missing.

"Well, well," said the visitor, "and why do you like this one best?"

"I love her most," said the little girl, "because if I didn't love her, no one else would."[3]

The beauty of Christmas is that God knew our condition: tattered lives, broken hearts, blind eyes, missing parts. If He didn't love us, no one else would. That's why He sent Jesus, not just as a babe in Bethlehem, but as a permanent companion for us—anytime, day or night.

Hello and Goodbye

The memory of the just is blessed.
PROVERBS 10:7 KJV

Famed mountain-folk singer and entertainer Jean Ritchie was performing for a gathering of college students at Lees McRae College in Banner Elk, North Carolina, in the late 1970s when she told this simple story that must have touched the hearts of everyone present that day:

> *My father recently passed away after a few years of health problems. The most notable of his problems was that he could not remember or recognize anyone in the family any longer. He was kind and gentle until he died and for that we are grateful, but it was so painful for my mom to live with a stranger who did not recognize her. My mom often remarked to me that she would*

love to have just one more conversation with my dad — a conversation where he remembered her and they could relive old times just once more.

A couple of days before my father passed away, he was coming down the hallway when my mom came barreling out of the bedroom and they smacked right into one another. With a start, my father said, 'Why Bessie, there you are! I have been looking all over for you.' They then enjoyed a lucid conversation for nearly fifteen minutes until my father's memory failed again, and with that my mom was able to accept his death more easily. In fact, she was grateful for the opportunity to say hello and goodbye to her husband of more than fifty years.

Holidays are similar to this. They provide each of us with a chance to say the things we should say but often don't, to forgive the things that need forgiving rather than ignoring, and to affirm one another's value rather than strive for one-upmanship.

Noodles on the Ceiling

And I will be quiet, and will be no more angry.
EZEKIEL 16:42 KJV

The move from a small town in northeastern Colorado to the city of Houston, Texas, had been difficult for the family. For one thing, the food was so different. But Christmas day was here, and preparations for a traditional "northern" dinner were nearing completion. They were going to have roast chicken with bread dressing, green beans, hot rolls, mashed potatoes, and homemade noodles.

The noodles were swimming in a buttery broth as Dad carried the bowl from the kitchen to the dining room. Just as he entered, one of the boys came around the corner at a dead run and hit Dad's right arm.

Things seemed to happen in slow motion then. The bowl tilted slightly as it fell, and being heavier than the noodles, it fell faster so that when the bowl hit the floor the noodles zoomed down one side of it and up the other, splattering all over the room—some even hanging from the ceiling.

Rather than become angry, Dad burst into laughter at the sight of those noodles stuck to the ceiling. Everyone pitched in, and soon the mess was cleaned up. Then the young family, lonesome and far from home, shared its first Christmas in the new place where God had brought them; a Christmas dinner that was blessed because of a dad who could see the humor in an accident rather than the mess of a mistake.

Do your best to see the humor of the situation when things grow tense during the holiday season. It will make a world of difference in the memories you create.

Faithful Saints

Let us not become weary in doing good, for at the proper time we will reap a harvest if we do not give up.
GALATIANS 6:9

Rev. B.C. Housewright, a retired minister, and his wife, Lottie, exited their car and began an arduous walk to the worship center. B.C. leaned on his cane and walked with a limp; he had recently been diagnosed with cancer. Lottie, bending forward, suffering with osteoporosis and other health problems, placed her hand on B.C.'s arm for stability. This couple, married for more than fifty-five years, had every reason to excuse themselves from attending church. But as long as they could, they came—jovial and overflowing with love, thankfulness, and enthusiasm for the Lord.

Two elderly people met Mary and Joseph when they brought Jesus to the temple in Jerusalem to be dedicated to God.

Simeon, a devout Jewish man, expected the Messiah to appear. The Scripture says, "The Holy Spirit was upon him" (Luke 2:25), and with that preview of Pentecost, Simeon scooped up Baby Jesus into his arms as he prophesied over the child. He knew the Messiah had come.

Anna, widowed after only seven years of marriage, had served in the temple for sixty years. When she saw the infant, she too recognized Him in her heart. Anna began worshipping and thanking God.

How uplifting these two affirming experiences must have been for young Mary and Joseph.

DEAR LORD,

Help us be more like Simeon and Anna and B. C. and Lottie. May we, too, become like these faithful servants who quietly, consistently, day-by-day served You, and believed Your promises.

AMEN.

No It Isn't

A quarrelsome person keeps an argument going.
PROVERBS 26:21 NCV

———————————

Mandy and Joe had been fighting all day. Now the young couple sat in stony silence at their church's Christmas pageant. When the lights dimmed, both stared straight ahead, their grudge still smoldering.

As the curtain opened, a golden retriever, who played the part of the donkey, was snuffling through bales of hay on the stage. A pillow-pregnant kindergartner marched next to an irritated first grader who kept pulling on the retriever's leash, trying to get to the door of the inn. When the retriever wouldn't budge, the resourceful first grader yelled, "Anybody home?"

"I am the innkeeper," came the stilted reply from a bespectacled boy. "What do you want?"

"We need a room," the first-grade Joseph answered. "Is your inn full?"

32

The bespectacled innkeeper stoutly replied, "No, it isn't."

This wasn't the expected answer. Joseph was confused, so he asked again. "Is your inn full?"

Again the innkeeper replied, "No, it isn't." The audience rustled in their seats.

The pillowed Mary informed the innkeeper,

"You're *supposed* to say the inn *is full!*" to which the innkeeper replied, "No, it isn't!" The audience began to chuckle.

In louder tones Mary and Joseph both bellowed, "Yes, it is!" only to hear the innkeeper say, just as loudly, "No, it isn't!" Before blows could be struck, the pastor's wife announced a brief recess.

Amid the audience's laughter, Mandy and Joe turned to each other with words of apology. And thereafter, whenever they found themselves feuding, one would say to the other, "No, it isn't" and the other would respond, "Yes, it is," remembering a Christmas pageant that ended an argument with laughter.

_____

Great with Child

Joseph also went . . . to be taxed with Mary his
espoused wife, being great with child.
LUKE 2:4-5 KJV

"U-Cut Christmas Trees!" the sign announced. Acres of trees spilled across the rolling, snow-covered hills. As soon-to-be parents, Bob and Sandy wanted this Christmas to be special. They parked their car by an old barn, took a saw from the nurseryman, and headed toward a stand of spruces.

Trudging through the snow was tiring, but finally Bob hollered, "I see a great tree. Come on!" The tree was perfectly shaped and tall enough for their ceiling, so they cut it, shouldered the saw, and began their trek back to the nurseryman's barn.

But Sandy was eight and a half months pregnant. She found that she had trouble wedging her bulk between the tree branches to get a good grip on its trunk to help carry it to the car. She ended up walking sideways, tripping over tree stumps, and twisting her ankles. By the time they wrestled the tree to the roof of the car, Sandy was exhausted. Bob finished tying their prize to the car as Sandy collapsed on the front seat.

Sighing heavily, Sandy remembered another very pregnant mother. Mary probably would have been more exhausted on her arrival in Bethlehem than Sandy was on her return to the parking lot. Yet Sandy had a warm apartment to go home to. Mary found only a stable. The complaints Sandy harbored about her twisted ankles dissolved into a thankful prayer for God's provision. Mary and Sandy were both "great with child," awaiting the arrival of God's best gift to them—a child. Though her feet ached, Sandy smiled. A baby *and* a Christmas tree. What a special Christmas this would be!

Family "His Tree"

*For the Mighty One has done great things for
me; and holy is His name. And His mercy is
upon generation after generation toward those
who fear Him.*
LUKE 1:49-50 NASB

While decorating the Christmas tree at Grandma's house, Helena held up a red tree skirt trimmed in white lace and asked, "What is this, Grandma?"

Grandma smiled and said, "That little tree skirt was a gift our landlady, Mrs. Ratcliffe, made and gave us the first year Granddad and I were married. She lived upstairs and we rented the downstairs part of her two-story house."

Helena pulled out an old glass ornament with blue paint peeling off. "Grandma, is this old?"

"Yes, sweetheart, it was one of our very first. We could afford only one box of assorted ornaments, and that is the only one left. That first year Granddad and I strung popcorn and cranberries to help decorate our

A sweater-clad teddy bear ornament sparked another memory. "Helena," Grandma continued, "I sewed a bathrobe for Granddad as my present to him, and he gave me a sweater. We loved each other so much; we felt rich and thankful. God's blessings kept us from even considering what we did not have."

"See this basketball ornament?" Grandma showed Helena. "It reminds me of when your daddy played basketball on the high school team and won lots of trophies."

"Here's Mickey Mouse!" Helena squealed with delight.

"Your dad bought the Mickey ornament on a family vacation to Disney World when he was in grade school."

Through sharing family history vignettes, Grandma gave Helena a sense of God's loving faithfulness from generation to generation, decorating "HisTree" with words of gratefulness and praise.

Light Your World

You are the light of the world. A city on a hill cannot he hidden. Neither do people light a lamp and put it under a bowl. Instead they put it on its stand, and it gives light to everyone in the house.
MATTHEW 5:14-15

A popular Christmas legend tells of an old cobbler and his wife who lived in a small village in Austria. Although poverty-stricken, the couple shared generously with others. Every night they placed a lighted candle in the window of their cottage—a sign of hospitality to any traveler needing shelter.

The next few years brought war and famine to the little village, but the cobbler and his wife seemed to suffer much less than their neighbors.

One evening on Christmas Eve, the townspeople gathered to discuss their situation. "There is something special about the cobbler and his wife. They are always spared our misfortunes. What are they doing differently from us?"

One villager said, "Let's put a candle in our windows, too. Maybe that's the secret."

The entire village lit up that night as candles shone brightly in the window of every home. Early on Christmas morning the next day, a messenger delivered good news to the village. War was over. Peace had come! The villagers were so grateful for this blessing that they gave thanks to God and vowed to keep lighted candles in their homes every Christmas Eve.

War still rages in many countries throughout our world—and in the hearts of many people. We who know the Light of the World can make a difference. We can let our light shine in the windows of our hearts, reflecting the glory of Christ and inviting others to find a shelter for their journey. For peace, true peace, can be found only in Him.

It's a Secret

*The gift of God is eternal life through Jesus
Christ our Lord.*
ROMANS 6:23 KJV

"Hey, Dad I bet you can't guess what I got you for Christmas," five-year-old Bobby hollered.

"Well, I am sure that I can't guess it unless you give me a hint," his dad replied.

"It's one of those things you stick on your tie," Bobby answered.

As his dad laughed, he heard a burst of exasperation from Bobby's mom come from the other room as she overheard Bobby give away the secret. It was obvious to everyone but Bobby that he had just told his dad to expect a tie tack for Christmas. A few nights later, on Christmas Eve, the gifts were opened, and Bobby grinned with delight as his father expressed great surprise when he opened his present and found a tie tack.

Holidays bring with them marvelous surprises and a sense of naïveté often missing from the more mundane aspects of our lives. We need to make sure that we invest in the magic of the holiday spirit as often as we can, and we need to be active participants in the glow that comes from believing in love for all times. In short, we need to find ways to engage one another in the pureness of giving and receiving from the heart rather than from the pocketbook.

Bobby's excitement came from the enjoyment his "secret" gift brought to his dad. His father's joy came from the love he experienced as his young son gave him something special.

God the Father is just like this. He knows the "secret" of what we are going to give Him even before we do; yet He is genuinely delighted when we do submit our lives to Him. And it is amazing just how much peace and contentment we experience then, because we know that we have pleased Him.

———————————

Festival of Lights

*Let your light shine before men in such a way
that they may see your good works, and glorify
your Father who is in heaven.*
MATTHEW 5:16 NASB

The menorah, a candelabra with four candles on each side and one in the middle, actually represents a miracle. It is used during the winter Jewish holiday known as Hanukkah or The Festival of Lights. Hanukkah, which means *dedication,* commemorates the revolt against the Syrian Greeks in 167-164 B.C., when the Jews recaptured the temple and rededicated it to God's service.

The Greeks had extinguished the great seven-branched candelabra in the temple, and only enough oil remained for the light to burn one day. It took eight days for the priests to consecrate more oil. Nevertheless, the Jews lit the lamp stand, and it continued to burn for eight full days!

Thus the Feast of Dedication, also called the Festival of Lights, was established. In Jewish homes the miniature menorah candles are lit, one each day, to represent the eight days. The center candle is the *shamash*, a Hebrew word meaning *servant,* and it is used to light the other candles. From Scripture, Christians know that Jesus is the Light of the World, God's *shamash*.[4]

The Jerusalem temple has been destroyed, but when we receive Christ, we become the temple of God and the *shamash* shines in our hearts. We become lights in a dark world. Through His Holy Spirit we have a never-ending supply of oil to keep our lamps brightly burning.

Unexpected Solo

I can do everything through him who gives me strength.
PHILIPPIANS 4:13

Virginia finished her lines and walked slowly on to the "Christmas on Main Street" stage. The rest of the "RingerSinger" choir was to join her to sing and ring hand bells. Virginia took her place with much more poise than was usual for a five-year-old.

The cue came for the choir to join Virginia. She looked left toward the stage door. Nothing happened. Her gaze went to her choir director on the front row. He nodded at her to begin. *Begin?* she thought. *But where are the others?*

Virginia's stomach was full of butterflies. Her eyes brimmed with tears. She was on stage before a thousand people. Alone. But the show must go on. Silently she asked God to help her. She began to sing, softly at first but then with more confidence. Her lone hand bell resonated at just the right moment. Slowly her mouth curved into a smile. She was actually enjoying being the star.

Halfway through the song, the rest of the choir rushed in. They had been given the wrong time to enter from backstage. Getting to their spots *quickly* seemed more important than getting to their spots *quietly!* Together they sang and rang the last few lines of "Ring the Bells."

Virginia never planned to sing a solo. At the performance the night before, everything had gone perfectly. The choir appeared on time and joined Virginia on stage. The audience had loved these twelve musically accomplished children.

Although the choir messed up at this performance, Virginia knew what was expected of her, and she didn't let the unexpected situation bother her. Wise beyond her years, she took her cue and sang. With God's help, she learned courage and confidence.

Warmth of the Sun

Again, if two lie together, then they have heat:
but how can one be warm alone?
ECCLESIASTES 4:11 KJV

How can one's love for another human being be so intense? Rob wondered as he looked at his wife of fifteen years finishing the Christmas wrapping.

Jane is truly the best thing that has ever happened to me. I don't know if you could say that I love her more now than I did when we first married, because I have always loved her more than I can imagine; but I certainly appreciate her more. She has stood by me during the lean times. She has encouraged me to "reach for the stars" career wise. And she has believed in me when I didn't know how to believe in myself. On top of all of that, she has shown me how to be gracious and kind through her devotion to serving others. What a wife she is!

It was late in the evening, and both of the kids were in bed asleep. Jane was wrapping small Christmas gifts she had purchased for each member of the pastoral staff and others with whom she worked. Earlier she had finished decorating the living room for Christmas by hanging the children's stockings and putting the finishing touches on the room decor. No lumps of coal would be found in Nicole and Brandons stockings — that's for sure!

The sense of peace was real, and Rob didn't want to do anything to disturb it. So he just continued to sit quietly and watch her work. Her presence touched something deep inside him and warmed him the same way a pleasant summer sun warms tired muscles and produces contentment. Rob silently prayed, *Thank You, Lord, for bringing her into my life!*

If we will pause in our hectic holiday schedules, we will find many moments for thanksgiving. The people God has brought into our lives to warm our hearts with His love are among the best blessings of all.

Shining Lights and Singing Angels

*Surely goodness and mercy shall follow me all
the days of my life: and I will dwell in the house
of the Lord for ever.*
PSALM 23:6 KJV

An Air Force sergeant in Thailand let his light shine. When others were out partying and chasing women, he stayed in, talked to the other soldiers, relaxed, and read.

One day, a young soldier asked him why. The sergeant shared his faith in God with the young man and told him that his relationship with Jesus meant he made different lifestyle choices. The two began reading scriptures together and praying regularly. The older soldier had the joy of leading the younger man to his Lord.

Christmas was approaching, and the young man celebrated his new birth as the world celebrated Christ's birth.

Due to seniority, the sergeant went home for holiday leave, while some of the others in the unit stayed behind, including the younger soldier. When the sergeant returned, the men in his unit met his plane with unhappy news. The young soldier had been killed in battle the day before.

Though deeply saddened by the passing of his young friend, the sergeant comforted the other soldiers with the truth of good news: "This year, he really did get to go 'home' for Christmas."

A great crowd of witnesses worships at God's throne. In endless praise, those who have gone on to be with our Lord in Heaven ahead of us can inspire hope in our hearts. Christmas is a special time to join in the heavenly celebration of joy.

Life's Ups and Downs

*I have learned to be content whatever the
circumstances.*
PHILIPPIANS 4:11

The highlight of every Christmas season was the trip to Uncle Bill's farm. Uncle Bill was a dairyman. Though he kept only a small herd, Uncle Bill's life revolved around the rhythms of farm life—early morning milking, chores, machinery repair, but also, fun! After a good snowfall, Uncle Bill would hitch his horse to an old box wagon equipped with a pair of sled runners. All of the visiting relatives would pile into the wagon. Then Uncle Bill would snap the reins, and off they'd go, cold wind painting their faces red, whistles and laughter echoing over the countryside.

Sometimes the wagon would slide around a bend and get stuck in a snowdrift. Then Uncle Bill would make everyone get out of the wagon. Someone would have to hold the horse's head while everyone else pushed. If anyone complained, Uncle Bill would remind him or her that you have to take the bad along with the good in life. Before they knew it, the wagon would be sledding down the road again with everyone whistling and laughing all the way home.

Uncle Bill knew that while good times are an occasion for happiness, bad times are a time to be content—not a time to moan, fret, or worry. God is still in control. We can trust Him, and soon, like the old sled wagon, everything will be back on track, and we'll be whistling and laughing all the way home.

Look Out for Leah

Thou shalt be a blessing.
GENESIS 12:2 KJV

It was the day after Christmas, and Bobby was visiting his older cousin at her family's home in Oklahoma. He had received a new bicycle for Christmas and was riding it in the neighborhood. He was a fairly small six-year-old and shy. A couple of neighborhood children decided they did not like having a strange kid riding up and down the streets, so they stopped him and threatened him.

They were around seven or eight years old, bigger than he, and Bobby ran inside crying. His cousin Leah, who was ten, decided something had to be done about the situation. Quickly she marched down the street, found the two young culprits, and as only a ten-year-old girl can do to smaller and younger boys, threatened them with severe consequences unless they were nice to her cousin. Contritely, the two boys apologized.

Leah had confirmed what Bobby always knew — she would look out for him and protect him whenever he needed her. It was a very comforting thought.

The joys of the holiday season come in many ways. One of these ways is in knowing that we all belong to a spiritual family that is close-knit and caring. Just as Leah stood up for Bobby in the face of a trial, we in God's family, must look out for one another. Not everyone is blessed with earthly family members who care and love them. But those who are can be ever mindful of the needs of others.

As scripture says, "From everyone who has been given much, much will be demanded" (Luke 12:48). Let's find ways to be a blessing to others. When we do, we are all richer for it.

Fear Not

And the angel said unto her, Fear not, Mary:
for thou hast found favor with God. And, behold,
thou shalt conceive in thy womb, and bring forth
a son, and shalt call his name JESUS.
L U K E   1 : 3 0 - 3 1   K J V

Elaine lived in a two-story, secluded country home filled with the sounds of laughter, the chatter of children playing, and delightful conversations with her husband of twenty-five years. Then everything changed. Her beloved husband died suddenly about the time their children moved away to college.

Different sounds Elaine had never noticed before were amplified, especially at night. An acorn dropping on the roof or squirrels bumping a tree limb near the house were reminders that she was alone. When her heart pounded and raced, Elaine overcame her fear by meditating on a favorite verse, "When I am afraid, I will put my trust in Thee" (Psalm 56:3 NASB). By concentrating on God's power and presence, Elaine could rest and feel His peace—a peace that passed her own understanding.

We can only imagine how terrified Mary must have felt when the angel came to her and said, "Fear not." Surely she must have worried about rejection from her parents, friends, and Joseph, not to mention her fears about becoming the mother of God's Son. Yet God's peace ruled in her heart as she said, "I am willing, Lord."

DEAR LORD,

Please help us remember that even when the unexpected happens, You are there. Help us, like Elaine, to concentrate on Your presence and Your Word. Help us, like Mary, to replace our fears with childlike faith, submission, and confidence in Your plans for our lives.

AMEN.

Happy Birthday, Jesus?

Let us fix our eyes on Jesus, the author and perfecter of our faith.
HEBREWS 12:2

It was the first day of December, the day Kerry's family always decorated for Christmas. She enlisted her husband Donny's help, and together they heaved the seasonal boxes down from the attic.

Working through one box at a time, Kerry and her family gingerly began one of their favorite traditions. While Donny assembled the artificial tree, the children selected their favorite items for display.

"I get the music boxes!" yelled seven-year-old Billy.

Fifteen-year-old Melissa dug deep in the box. "I'll put up the wreaths!"

"Give me the manger scene—and Baby Jesus," added Sarah, their preschooler. "I know right where they go!"

Together they unwrapped all the boxes and decorated the tree until every ornament and light shimmered in its place.

"Mama!" Sarah wailed. "Where's Baby Jesus? Here's the wise men, the sheep, the camels, the shepherds. Here's Mary and Joseph and the manger. But Jesus is missing! I've looked everywhere!"

The family searched carefully through the boxes but found nothing. "I'm sorry, Sarah," soothed Kerry. "Maybe He will turn up somewhere."

"But it's His birthday! And He's not even here!"

Christmas arrived, and the family members forgot about the missing person in the Nativity. A few days later, Kerry was sorting through the Christmas boxes and returning each item to its proper place. Wrapped up in a wad of tissue paper at the bottom of one box, she found the ceramic replica of Baby Jesus.

A Christmas party without the guest of honor? How easy it is to lose perspective in the wrappings and trappings of the season and forget to honor the very one we're celebrating.

_____

Something to Remember

Remember the former things of old,
for I am God, and there is no other.
ISAIAH 46:9 NKJV

Grandma came from the "old country." She spoke with a thick accent and often struggled to find the right English words when she shared about her faith in God. But Grandma could cook! And when Christmastime came around, Grandma's house was filled with the delicious aromas of her Christmas breads and rolls.

As the years passed, Grandma succumbed to painful arthritis in her hands and shoulders. Though she could no longer knead the dough used in her Christmas rolls, Grandma still could share her faith.

One year Grandma asked her granddaughter to come for a visit. Grandma wanted to make her Christmas rolls one last time. Using the granddaughter's hands and Grandma's expertise, the two women worked together, kneading the dough and stuffing the rolls while Grandma kept saying, "Remember this . . . do this."

That night, before she went to sleep, the granddaughter carefully wrote down all of the ingredients and reviewed all of the steps in making Grandma's rolls so that she could remember how to make them the following year. And she did. And she still does. Now every Christmas she teaches her children and grandchildren how to make Grandma's Christmas rolls, filling her kitchen with the same delicious aromas that filled her grandma's kitchen long ago.

But the granddaughter shares more than a recipe and special Christmas rolls to feed her hungry family. She also shares Grandma's lessons of faith and trust in God.

Grandma's rolls may fill an empty stomach, but Grandma's faith could fill an empty heart. Now that's something to remember!

A Change of Direction

The shepherds went back, glorifying and praising
God for all that they had heard and seen, just as
had been told them.
L U K E   2 : 2 0   N A S B

Two couples on vacation rented a car to drive on the backroads of beautiful British Columbia. Jim and Fran sat in the front; and Fran's mother, Billie, and her stepdad, Dobber, sat in the back.

Jim was driving along when they saw a dirt road angling to the right with the correct highway number posted. Fran said, "Surely that isn't the main road. Maybe the sign was turned. Look, the road straight ahead is paved and lined with utility poles, too."

After a lighthearted discussion, the couples took a vote and decided to stay on what appeared to be the main highway. After a few miles, Jim drove up a little hill, and then suddenly all they could see was water, a few small buildings, and a campground sign. The road came to a dead end there at a lovely lake and campsite. The couples began laughing as Jim wheeled the car around and headed back to the dirt road turn they had missed. Eventually, the humble highway meandered into the most magnificent scenery of all.

At Christmastime, we could stay on the broad, paved road and mindlessly travel to the dead end of shopping, tinsel, and plastic. Or we could, like the shepherds, change our thinking and our plans, turn down the narrow road to Bethlehem, and worship the newborn King. Which will you choose?

———————————————

A Gift of Love

Give, and it will be given to you. A good
measure, pressed down, shaken together and
running over, will be poured into your lap.
LUKE 6:38

Kids made fun of "old woman Smith."

"Everyone knows she's crazy!" they said.

"She's NOT crazy," Tessie defended repeatedly. "Maybe she doesn't have any family. Maybe she's just lonely."

"But she claims people try to steal her money."

"She's poor like us. Just look at her run-down house and the filth in her yard."

"And she's grumpier then my bulldog!"

But Tessie ignored their taunts and adopted Mrs. Smith as her own special project. All through the year, she picked up trash and pulled her neighbor's weeds. In spring she planted flowers in her yard. She ran errands for the old woman and visited her daily.

Never once did Mrs. Smith say "thank you." And no one else seemed to care. Only once did Tessie see a stranger, a middle-aged man, enter the widow's house.

On Christmas Eve, Tessie took Mrs. Smith a basket of fruit and a special handmade gift. When no one answered the door, Tessie cautiously peered in, calling out her name softly.

Inside on the living room couch lay Mrs. Smith. She apparently had died in her sleep. In her lap was a small, unwrapped Christmas present.

Tessie, her mom, and one man attended the woman's funeral—the same man Tessie had seen at Mrs. Smith's house a few weeks earlier.

The man handed Tessie the box she had seen in the old woman's lap. "I'm Mrs. Smith's lawyer," he said.

Tessie opened the box, and inside was a cashier's check to her for $100,000, along with a note: "For college education first. Then spend wisely—as you wish."

Henry Wadsworth Longfellow said, "Give what you have. To someone it may be better than you dare to think." Giving out of love may not make us wealthy, but the return investment will be more than we give away—always.

Joy to the World

The joy of the Lord is your strength.
NEHEMIAH 8:10 NASB

Music had always been a vital part of the young mother's life, but the Christmas following the death of her baby son, she did not feel like singing. Her Bible study group had decided to go Christmas caroling, urging her to join them. The emptiness of a grieving mother's heart seemed too deep. She thought it would be impossible to sing and cry at the same time.

But with the gentle prompting of a few friends and the loving encouragement of her husband, the young mother joined the caroling group. As she studied the faces of the lonely people in the nursing homes and the elderly shut-ins, she stopped thinking of herself and her grief. In some of those eyes she saw joy and peace. In others, she detected pain and sorrow. She felt compassion for them and a desire to share the wonders of God's love, the same love and grace that were sustaining her through the most difficult time of her life.

When she sang "Joy to the World," she meant it. She realized that while Christmas may not be a happy time for many families for various reasons, true joy is a matter of the heart. The grieving mother was uplifted because she focused her attention upon others. She was comforted by the thought that someday she would be with her son once again in heaven.

DEAR JESUS,

Sometimes it seems I can't go on.
But thank You, Lord, You give me a song.
Joy in the night, courage by day,
Strength for each moment along the way.

AMEN.

For the Least of These

No one has ever seen God; but if we love one another, God lives in us and his love is made complete in us.

1 JOHN 4:12

In Henry Van Dyke's classic, *The Other Wise Man*, Artaban plans to join his three friends in Babylon as they followed the star in search of the King. He has three jewels to offer as gifts to the Christ Child.

But before he arrives, Artaban finds a feverish, poor Hebrew exile in the road. Torn between duty and desire, he ultimately stays and ministers for hours to the dying man. By the time Artaban arrives at the Bethlehem stable, the other Magi have left. A note encourages him to follow them through the desert.

But Artaban has given the dying man his last provisions, so he returns to the city, sells one of his three jewels, and buys camels and food. In the deserted town of Bethlehem, a frightened woman cradling her baby tells Artaban that Joseph, Mary, and the Babe fled to Egypt to escape Herod's soldiers who are killing all the baby boys in the city. He offers a ruby to one of Herod's soldiers to save the woman's child.

Heartbroken that he has spent two of his gifts already, Artaban wanders for years seeking to worship the new King. He discovers no Baby King but finds many poor, sick, and hungry to feed, clothe, and comfort.

Many years later in Jerusalem, white-haired Artaban hears about a king being executed. He rushes toward Calvary to ransom the king with his last jewel. But instead, Artaban ends up rescuing a young woman from slavery.

At the end of the story, Artaban laments the turn of events. He wanted to bring gifts and minister to the King of kings. Yet he spent his fortune helping people in need. The Lord comforts him with these words: "Verily I say unto you, inasmuch as ye have done it unto one of the least of these my brethren, ye have done it unto me" (Matthew 25:40 KJV).

The celebration of Christmas is more than just a holiday. And worship is more than mere words or gifts. Like the fourth wise man learned, real worship is a way of life.

A Sacrificial Stocking

Do not forget to do good and to share with others, for with such sacrifices God is pleased.
HEBREWS 13:16

Nancy had always had a Christmas stocking. It wasn't fancy. It didn't have her name on it at the top. In fact, it wasn't much more than a knee sock that had lost its stretch. But every year that unexceptional sock was filled on Christmas Day with candy, treats, and a coin or two.

This year was different. This year Nancy was married and would be spending Christmas several thousand miles away from her childhood home. She was a grown woman, yet Nancy missed that old knee sock and the memories it held. When her husband asked why she looked so sad, Nancy told him about the sock. Wiping her tears and shrugging, she assured him that it was a silly, ugly, old sock anyway.

However, on Christmas morning, there in her favorite chair was a Christmas stocking! It wasn't fancy. It didn't have her name on it at the top. It was something better! Using pieces of her old Christmas knee sock and some pieces from a neighbor's scrap bag, Nancy's husband had made a patchwork Christmas stocking. He had worked late after she had gone to bed, cutting and sewing and tearing out his mistakes.

As he laughingly related the difficulties involved in making that Christmas stocking, Nancy smiled and silently thanked God for her husband's sacrificial love. She was pleased, and she knew that God was, too.

Years later, Nancy still hangs that patchwork stocking. It's her reminder to find ways to do good for others, even if it means a sacrifice of time and effort. Even ugly old knee socks can represent hope and joy.

_____

The Inside Story

And the Word became flesh, and dwelt among
us, and we beheld His glory, glory as of the only
begotten from the Father, full of grace and truth.
JOHN 1:14 NASB

While visiting Amsterdam, Holland, an American couple happened upon the old Westkirke Church, the tallest building in the city. The couple stopped and joined a group outside, thinking they would be touring the church, but their tour was of the bell tower. The couple adventurously climbed about eight stories of steps, narrow spiral staircases, and finally a ladder. Their guide stopped along the way to explain how the different-sized bells were played.

He said, "Only six men in the city know how to play this organ-like instrument which chimes the bells."

Pointing to one corner, he said, "Notice the heavy wooden beams in each angle of the tower. These absorb the enormous vibrations of the heavy bells and keep the bricks from crumbling."

Later in the day, the couple could hear bells ringing from the tower off in the distance. They stopped and listened. The sounds meant more since they could imagine the man inside the tower busily shifting ropes and wooden slats and maneuvering around in that small space. The sounds were richer and more meaningful.

Bells are often painted on Christmas cards and decorations during the holiday season, but they never quite capture the beauty of the real ones. Likewise, we may hear about the Christmas story, but only when we know Jesus Himself will our hearts truly resonate with the joy the chimes proclaim during the holiday season.

———————————

The Twelve Days of Giving

Freely you have received, freely give.
MATTHEW 10:8

Patricia Moss listened to her children whine and cry in the toy department over which toy they'd get at Christmas and watched the pushing and shoving of the department store crowds. Then she stepped back for a minute to examine her family's values.

She decided to adopt a friend's tradition originating from the song, "The Twelve Days of Christmas." Beginning early in fall, she would try to pick a family that might need encouragement to get into the Christmas spirit. Then twelve days before Christmas, she and her family would begin slipping anonymous gifts onto the front porch of that family. They would write cute poems to go with the gifts, such as, "Twelve days before Christmas, a true friend gave

72

to me, twelve candy canes, to hang upon the tree." The eleventh day before Christmas might be eleven fancy bows, the tenth day, a "tin" of ten giant homemade cookies, on and on right up to Christmas day.

One year the Moss family chose an elderly man who had suffered a stroke. He and his wife had decided not to put up a tree that year until the "twelve days" gifts started arriving. Another year they selected two families to cheer because both sons had friends whose families needed their love and care.

Patricia said that even after her sons were grown and had moved away, they still participated in this tradition when they returned home for Christmas.[5]

Patricia taught her children well, allowing them a hands-on opportunity not only to *see* good, but also to *do* good, moving them beyond their own problems as they gave generously of themselves to others.

_____

Little Blessings

I will extol the Lord at all times;
his praise will always be on my lips.
PSALM 34:1

Janice smiled as she took her seat near the back. The Christmas concert had begun before she could get there from work. Immediately she felt drawn into the spirit of the season with the beautiful music of the concert choir.

The choir was dressed in green and white and flanked by red poinsettias and gold bows. They looked like they could have come straight from the front of a Christmas card. But Janice didn't linger long on the big picture. Her focus went immediately to a lovely young girl in the middle of the back row. Polly sang with obvious joy. Halfway through the song, Janice's and Polly's eyes met, and they both smiled. Without missing a note, Polly raised one eyebrow in a silent salute to her mother.

No one else in the auditorium knew what had transpired. But in that instant, Janice had been intensely blessed by her daughter.

Often Janice was tired from working a full-time job. But Polly always seemed to sense when she needed a little extra encouragement. It frequently came in a very inconspicuous way, maybe a raised eyebrow, a pat on the back, or an *I Love You* scribbled on a scrap piece of paper.

Most of us have overloaded calendars. Often just the smallest moment of acknowledgement blesses our entire day. Perhaps today you might find a way to be that special blessing to someone else. Remember, sometimes it's the little things that mean the most.

Polished Thanks

In all you do, give thanks to God.
COLOSSIANS 3:17 NCV

As the pipe organ thundered out the notes to a favorite Christmas carol, stained-glass windows reflected the flickering of tiny candles at the church's Christmas Eve program. It should have put Maggie in the Christmas spirit, but all she could see was the dust and dirt and mess she would have to help clean up after this late-night service.

Maggie's grandfather was the church custodian. He needed extra help to keep the church clean at Christmastime, so Maggie and her siblings had been drafted to work with him. Trash would have to be collected, floors washed, and the white pews wiped clean of dirty handprints and boot marks before services the next day. Here Maggie was, stuck in an emptying church with a polishing cloth in her hand, wishing she could be anywhere else in the world. With a sigh she began to polish the pews.

Grandpa noticed her work and said with a smile, "God must be hearing a lot of thanksgiving from you." When she didn't reply or look up from her polishing, Grandpa continued, "With every push of the broom or every shovel of snow, I thank God for my job, don't you?"

Maggie didn't want Grandpa to know that she was more resentful than thankful that night. But she knew in her heart that he was right. "I'm sorry, God," she muttered. And by the time Maggie finished polishing the row, she had found that she could thank God — even for a job polishing pews. The next morning, as the sun blazed through the colored windows and reflected off her polished pews, Maggie said "thanks" once more — and smiled.

Miracles Still Happen

With man this is impossible,
but with God all things are possible.
MATTHEW 19:26

A small preschooler waited impatiently as the long "North Pole" line snaked its way to the department store Santa. Finally, the child arrived at the head of the line. He climbed in Santa's lap, eager to express his wish list.

Santa's blue eyes twinkled as his burly arms wrapped around the young child. "And what do you want Santa to bring you?" he asked. "A toy truck? A new football? A bike?"

The little boy shook his head no. "I want a new daddy," he whispered.

"What do you mean, 'a new daddy'?"

"I want my daddy to act different. My daddy does drugs." A tear trickled down the preschooler's face.

Santa tried to console the child and promised his best, knowing he could not provide this impossible request.

Jim Cymbala, author of *Fresh Wind, Fresh Fire* and pastor of the inner city Brooklyn Tabernacle in New York, shows a video of one young man in his church. In that clip, the young man explains how he often left his wife and children for days, living in a literal dog house while nurturing his crack addiction.

One night his wife and children had gone to Pastor Cymbala's church, where many of the people began to pray earnestly for the woman's husband. That night, as if drawn by some unseen power, the young addict made his way to the church. As he walked down the aisle of the massive building, he heard his name spoken aloud in a petition to God. He knelt at the church altar and gave his life to Christ. He abandoned his habit and soon began singing in church and ministering to others.

Two stories—different endings. What seems impossible for us is always possible for God. Miracles still happen—and not just at Christmastime.

———————————

A Father's Hymn

"Peace, peace, to those far and near," says the
Lord. "And I will heal them."
ISAIAH 57:19

History books record the suffering that befell families during the American Civil War. Many families were touched by the profound losses of life, damage to property, or reversals of fortune that accompanied the conflict.

Among the survivors of that dreadful war was a young man named Charley. When he left his home to serve as a soldier in the Union Army, Charley was convinced of his invincibility and emboldened by his ideals. But before the conflict was over, Charley returned home, wounded but alive. His arrival coincided with the beginnings of the Christmas holidays, and his father, Henry Wadsworth Longfellow, penned the lines of "I Heard the Bells on Christmas Day" in his honor.

Longfellow's words echo the cry of every heart that longs for "peace on earth." And though this father's hymn reverberates with the heartache that accompanies the hardships of life, it ends with the assurance that God is not dead, and His peace will prevail.

I heard the bells on Christmas Day,
Their old familiar carols play:
And wild and sweet The words repeat,
Of peace on earth, good will to men.
But in despair, I bowed my head.
"There is no peace on earth," I said.
"For hate is strong
"And mocks the song
"Of peace on earth, good will to men."
Then pealed the bells more loud and deep,
"God is not dead, nor doth He sleep.
"The wrong shall fail;
"The right prevail,
"With peace on earth, good will to men."[6]

The Second Mile

Go with him two miles.
MATTHEW 5:41

Dale Galloway loves to tell a story he heard about Dwight L. Moody and his Sunday school in Chicago. A little boy named Johnny arrived late one cold January Sunday morning. His legs were blue from bitter winds blowing across Lake Michigan. He wore a tattered coat that was pulled together at the top with a safety pin. Johnny had no hat to keep his head warm, and his sock-less feet wore shoes that had holes in the bottom.

A Sunday school greeter saw the young boy enter the church and scooped him up in her arms, massaging the boy's half-frozen legs to start circulation again. A few minutes later, she sat the boy down and asked him where he lived. When the little boy responded, the greeter realized that home was more than two miles away. He had walked across the windy city of Chicago on a freezing January morning just to attend the

Sunday school of Dwight L. Moody—a walk where the cold can literally take away your breath and endanger your life.

"Why did you do it?" asked the friendly greeter. "There must have been a dozen churches that you walked past to come here. Why did you do it?"

The little boy was shy and hesitated a moment before he blurted out, "I guess, Ma'am, it is because they love a fellow over here."[7]

People know the difference between fake and real love. And those who don't mind "going the extra mile" to give love will find others walking the distance to receive it as well.

Christmas is about caring.

————————————

Joseph's Divine Assignment

Joseph also went up from Galilee, from the city of Nazareth, to Judea, to the city of David, which is called Bethlehem, because he was of the house and family of David, in order to register, along with Mary, who was engaged to him, and was with child.

LUKE 2:4-5 NASB

In her classic book, *Two from Galilee,* Marjorie Holmes paints a poignant word picture of the human drama that unfolded from the time the virgin Mary fell in love with Joseph until Jesus was born. How deeply Joseph loved Mary, yet the staggering reality of her becoming pregnant apart from their physical union became an issue with both their families. Did their parents believe them? Did Joseph believe Mary?

Can you imagine the inner struggles that Joseph felt? But after the angel's visit, Joseph knew that Mary was telling the truth. He took her as his wife but did not consummate the marriage until after Jesus' birth. Joseph did not seem bitter or revengeful. He just wanted to do the honorable thing. Joseph was a man of great integrity.

As a young man, he received the awesome assignment to become the earthly father of God's only begotten Son. With no parenting guidebook for his unique role, he simply had to trust his Heavenly Father to show him the way. Joseph was a man of great faith.

His faith gave way to action. When the angel later told Joseph to flee with Mary and Baby Jesus, he did not argue or give excuses. They left for Egypt right away. His prompt obedience indicated he walked closely with God and knew His voice.

Emmanuel Is Here

Behold, a virgin shall be with child, and shall bring forth a son, and they shall call his name Emmanuel, which being interpreted is, God with us.

MATTHEW 1:23 KJV

Two missionaries, captured by bandits and shut up in a filthy hole without fire, were miserably cold. To make things worse, the guard ordered them not to talk, not even to make signs to each other.

Christmas came. One of the missionaries, shivering and silent, sat on the floor. His face suddenly lit up, for he thought of a way to communicate with his comrade. Idly toying with bits of hay around him, he spelled out a word on the hard-packed mud. With a glance, he drew his friend's attention to it.

Immediately the friend's face brightened with triumphant joy. For the straws on the mud spelled out Emmanuel! What if they were captives of the bandits?

What if in peril of death? What if their prison was dirty and frigid?

Inwardly they exulted, "God is with us everywhere and at all times!"[8]

Janie felt the same way — imprisoned and alone in her home — until a neighbor knocked frantically on her door one Christmas Eve. Cradling her toddler, the woman begged to use Janie's phone. "My daughter . . . is choking!"

Janie held the baby, while the mother called 9-1-1.

God, are You here? Janie whispered. That's when she remembered the CPR training she had learned a few months earlier. Janie quickly dislodged a piece of chicken caught in the baby's throat.

The young mother was so grateful that she invited Janie to share Christmas dinner with them the next day.

We may never encounter circumstances like these, but we all face hopeless situations at times. Remembering the truth of Christmas — Emmanuel, God Is with Us — paints hope on the canvas of our hearts and renews courage even in the worst of times.

I cannot doubt, I will not doubt —
God With Us — He's near;
My prison walls bring freedom;
Emmanuel is here.

REBECCA BARLOW JORDAN[9]

Unspoken Love

We love because he first loved us.
1 JOHN 4:19

Christmas was approaching. Not known for his generosity, Andy had insisted he and Paula dispense with Christmas gifts for each other that year.

"After forty years together, what do we possibly need?" he said. "We'll just give the kids and grandkids a little money — easy all the way around."

Paula agreed reluctantly. She had learned through the years that arguing with Andy to abandon his Scrooge mentality never accomplished anything. His extravagant surprises through the years had been minimal. Once he had "splurged" and bought Paula a new washing machine for Christmas. Yet Paula knew he loved her. He just showed it other ways.

Besides, this year Andy's health concerned her more than Christmas gifts. He was losing a two-year battle with leukemia.

Christmas passed and, over the next six months, Andy's condition worsened. After several trips to the emergency room and three hospital stays, Andy passed away.

The first Christmas after his death was the worst for Paula. She retreated like a hermit and refused to put up a tree. Her children tried to encourage her, but she showed no interest.

On Christmas Eve, the doorbell rang. The local florist handed Paula two dozen roses. On the card she read the words: "To My Beloved Paula, the fragrance of my life. Forgive me for never telling you enough. Love, Andy."

But how . . . why? After Christmas Paula called the florist, who explained Andy's instructions. "Andy knew death was near. He arranged just before he died for us to send a different bouquet to you every month for a year, beginning with Christmas."

Coming to grips with our mortality has a sobering effect. Life is too short to "Scrooge" our way through it, for "love seeks not limits but outlets." How have you shown your love today?

Ready for Christmas

Prepare the way for the Lord.
MARK 1:3

———————————

Mike works for the production arm of a large retail chain of stores. He oversees the seasonal products for the gift and impulse areas of the stores. Mike has to make sure that each store is fully stocked with the right merchandise at the right time. What customer would want to buy Valentine's Day cards in the middle of back-to-school season or Mother's Day gifts at Thanksgiving time? If Mike does his job right, seasonal products are available in the stores at the right time of year.

To make sure that the product arrives on store shelves when customers expect it, Mike has to begin production of these items twelve to eighteen months in advance. When the product has been manufactured, he has to determine how many pieces of each product will go to each store. Those decisions have to be completed four to six months before the specific holiday. That means that Mike has to make all of his decisions about what each store will carry for back-to-school sales early in April. He has to order Easter products in November. And he has to choose products for Christmas by July 1. In fact, Mike hangs Christmas decorations and plays Christmas music in his office in early June to get him in the Christmas spirit.

We may not have all of our Christmas preparations ready by mid-summer like Mike does.

But we can avoid the last-minute rush that sometimes takes over during this busy season. With some realistic planning, we can be ready for Christmas —in our homes and in our hearts—and remember the reason for this season: God's wonderful gift of His Son.

———————————

The Baby Buggy Blues

Trust in the Lord with all your heart, and do not lean on your own understanding. In all your ways acknowledge Him, and He will make your paths straight.
PROVERBS 3:5-6 NASB

Thee pink plastic buggy with large white wheels came in a box labeled "Easy to Assemble." Thinking his four-year-old daughter's toy would take only a few minutes to put together, Jim spent most of Christmas Eve visiting with relatives. About midnight, Jim began working on the buggy.

The instructions were not very clear. Soon a teenaged nephew with computer science talents and another nephew with physics engineering skills joined their uncle to tackle the "easy task." All experienced the frustrations of small, ill-fitting screws, nuts, and bolts. Finally, at 3 am, the buggy was ready to roll. The exhausted trio fell into bed and had two full hours of sleep before the children awoke bright-eyed at 5:00 am, eager to open the gifts under the tree.

Squeals of delight became their payment when Angie saw the doll carriage. It would be difficult to estimate the miles it rolled, but that pink doll buggy always came to mind when anyone brought up a do-it-yourself project. It won the prize for the "one that almost defeated all the family geniuses."

DEAR FATHER,

Thank You that You have given us the Bible, our error-free blueprint for living. Thank You that Your wisdom is greater than our own. Forgive us when we try to figure out everything without asking You first. Help us remember that in spiritual matters, do-it-yourself projects always fail.

AMEN.

Are You Following Your Star?

After they had heard the king, they went on their
way, and the star they had seen in the east went
ahead of them until it stopped over the place
where the child was. When they saw the star,
they were overjoyed.
MATTHEW 2:9-10

"What's wrong with this wise man?" Hollace asked. "He has red spots all over him."

"I thought you would know what was the matter with him," said Aunt Linda. "He has the chicken pox just like you."

Hollace laughed. Four-year-old Hollace collects wise men, and each year he adds new ones to his collection. Little Hollace knows more about the wise men than do most adults. He knows Gaspar, Melchior, and Balthazar by name, how they traveled, and which gifts they brought to Baby Jesus. At bedtime, he only wants to hear books about the wise men.

Once Aunt Linda showed Hollace a new nativity scene she had bought. It was a small one-piece plastic figure with Mary, Joseph, Baby Jesus, a palm tree, and a few sheep. He immediately said, "The Wise Men aren't here. Aunt Linda, where are the Wise Men?"

While Aunt Linda searched for a logical answer that would make sense to a four-year-old, Hollace answered his own question. "Oh, I know where they are. They are following the star."

Many Christmas cards and plaques make the statement "Wise men still seek Him." Wise men followed the star to find the King of kings. We are still seekers today, and if we follow God's light, it will take us right to the Savior.

———————————————

The Great Exchange

Christ Jesus . . . didn't claim special privileges.
Instead, he lived a selfless, obedient life and then
died a selfless, obedient death.
PHILIPPIANS 2:5,8 MSG

Caballero, a forty-two-year-old triathlete and oilfield employee, was working at a petroleum well. Suddenly a pressure-regulating device that had not been properly installed exploded at a force that struck John at up to 2000 pounds per square inch.

The blast threw this fifteen-year industry worker thirty feet into a stand of pipes. The result? Brain damage, vision and hearing loss, a broken neck and back, a crushed foot and ankle, a dislocated hip, and he was literally scalped. Doctors said his prime physical condition helped him survive.

Accidents like this are not rare in such a volatile industry, but Caballero's response to the incident is a rare example of selflessness. The company involved was held accountable for the carelessly installed pressure device. A jury compensated Caballero for his medical expenses and lost earnings and awarded a $30,000,000 settlement to discourage future carelessness by any company in the industry. However, Caballero chose to reject the generous award—-in exchange for a company agreement to implement a safety plan that would protect other employees.

In Craig McDonald's newspaper article, he says, "John Caballero's life has been changed forever. While he is blessed to have his wife of twenty years and two children by his side, he will never work or compete in triathlons again. This ex-serviceman and model employee can never even throw a football with his children. No award, not even $30 million, could compensate him for his losses. But his first concern is still for others."[10]

At Christmas, the Son of God surrendered His throne rights in heaven and became a man, submissive even to His death thirty-three years later. Why? To award humanity with the unlimited riches of His Father's kingdom—and implement a plan that would change and protect their lives forever.

All because of love.

The Power of Faith

Without faith no one can please God.
HEBREWS 11:6 NCV

Jessie was three years old. Though her father had Been out of work for a long time, Jessie's mother smiled and said, "God will take care of us." When her father was offered a job with a small firm located halfway across the country, Jessie's mother smiled and said again, "God will take care of us." And though the move meant leaving relatives and friends behind, Jessie's mother told her with a smile, "God will take care of us."

When Jessie's family finally reached the town where they were going to live, they could not find a place to stay. It was Christmastime, and snow had been falling for days. Travelers were stranded; all of the hotels were full.

Tired and discouraged, Jessie's family turned down a side street and saw a brightly lit sign advertising a special Christmas program that evening at a nearby church. Jessie's mother began to cry, remembering the Christmas program that their relatives and friends back home would be enjoying this year without them. As she wept into her open hands, little Jessie leaned over, gave her mother a gentle kiss, and whispered, "God will take care of us."

Through tear-stained eyes, Jessie's mother looked up and gave Jessie a small smile. "You're right, sweetheart," she sniffled. Together the weary young family wandered into the small church and found themselves immediately engulfed in the welcoming warmth of the congregation. Before the program ended that evening, Jessie's family not only had a place to stay, but also a place to celebrate Christmas. Indeed, God *did* take care of them.

_____

Great Gift, Great Love

This is how God showed his love among us:
He sent his one and only Son into the world
that we might live through him.
1 JOHN 4:9

The story is told of a missionary who was once teaching a tribe in Africa about Christmas. "Christians," he said, "give gifts to others as an expression of their joy. In giving to others, they celebrate Christ's birthday and the gift that He is to mankind."

The missionary probably wondered if his teachings were clearly understood. He needn't have worried.

On Christmas morning, one of the natives presented the missionary with a beautiful seashell. When asked where he had discovered such an extraordinary shell, the native said he had walked many miles to a certain bay, the only spot where such shells could be found.

"I think it was wonderful of you to travel so far to get this lovely gift for me," the teacher exclaimed.

His eyes brightening, the native replied, "Long walk, part of gift."[11]

In the familiar Christmas story *Gift of the Magi,* a poor couple wanted to give each other a special gift. The woman decided to sell her beautiful, long hair, the pride of her life, to buy a fine watch chain for her husband's prized pocket watch. In the meantime, the husband, unaware of his wife's sacrifice, sold his watch to buy a set of beautiful, jeweled combs for his wife's hair. On Christmas day, they presented their selfless gifts, only to realize the irony of what they had done. They, too, might agree with the African student in their own words, "Big sacrifice, part of gift."

The greatest story of Christmas, the story that never grows old, the story that forever will be told, is that of a loving Father who gave His only Son as a gift to all—even to those who would never receive Him or appreciate it.

If asked why, perhaps God would answer, "Great love, part of gift."

My Daddy Fixed Me

*For you have not received a spirit of slavery
leading to fear again, but you have received a
spirit of adoption as sons by which we cry out,
"Abba! Father!"*
ROMANS 8:15 NASB

The company had gathered, all the children were playing outdoors, and Fran had just put the final trimmings on the Christmas feast. She was almost ready to reach for the dinner bell when a young boy with a frightened look on his face ran to the door and yelled, "Come quick! Steve got hurt."

Fran called to her husband, Jim, and together they ran out to the end of the paved driveway where their two-and-a-half-year-old son, Steve, had catapulted off a rolling plastic horse and landed on his chin. He had a gaping wound that would require stitches to heal.

The couple expressed regrets to their guests about the mealtime delay, picked up their crying child, jumped in the car, and headed for the hospital emergency room. When they arrived, restraining the tot was the worst part. With the child still howling, his medical doctor dad carefully applied local anesthetic to Steve's chin and sutured the cut. After the procedure was completed, Steve hopped off the table, took the red candy sucker offered by the nurse, and without a tear in his eyes, proudly announced, "My daddy fixed me!"

———————————

DEAR LORD,

At Christmastime so many people are aware of hurts and pains — both physical and emotional. Thank You that You are the Great Physician we can call upon in our distress. Thank You that You are our Abba, our Daddy. Thank You for healing us and binding up our wounds.

AMEN.

Gathered Again

Your children will return to their own land.
JEREMIAH 31:17

On any given day in December, stand beside a busy interstate and count the number of cars that whiz by. Wander through a bus or train station to glimpse at waiting areas and restaurants crowded with travelers. Look up to see the "friendly skies" filled with airplanes that are crammed with passengers. Where are all of these people going? Without a doubt some are traveling to be someplace with someone they love for Christmas.

Charles Dickens felt that only Christmas can "win us back to the delusions of our childish days, recall to the old man the pleasure of his youth, and transport the traveler back to his own fireside and quiet home!" Dickens knew that there was something comforting about gathering at a beloved place at Christmastime. It may be the sights and sounds of home. It may involve certain traditions or rituals. It may include sumptuous smells and favorite foods. Whatever the reason, many travelers choose to endure delays, crowded conditions, frayed tempers, and endless lines just so that they can be somewhere special for Christmas.

If you're traveling this season, here are some ABC's to make your trip easier:

- *Always check your travel arrangements — seat assignments, departure times, baggage restrictions, etc.*

- *Be prepared to wait — bring magazines, books, crossword puzzles, card games, etc.*

- *Carry a snack — a bottle of water, some fruit, a candy bar, cookies, or dry cereal in a throw-away container.*

- *Don't forget to smile. It's Christmas — Christ's birthday — so have a good time and a safe trip![12]*

Live Nativity

For God so loved the world, that He gave His
only begotten Son, that whoever believes in Him
should not perish, but have eternal life.
JOHN 3:16 NASB

Ridgecrest Baptist Church in Greenville, Texas, holds an annual live nativity in their community. The pageant has become a local tradition and received recognition by *Texas Highways Magazine*. Charter members of the church sew elaborate costumes to depict the nativity characters. Each participant stands motionless for one-half hour before being replaced by the next shift of folks dressed in identical costumes.

One year the nativity committee decided to take the scene to the Crossroads shopping mall across the street from the church. The shepherds entered from the north entrance, the wise men from the south, and the holy family, Mary, Joseph, and the infant Jesus, from the east. They converged in a central open area and assumed their positions.

Bonnie, the nativity director that year, said, "I was so surprised when a mother and her two children spontaneously approached the manger. Then what happened was so touching. There in the busy mall, the three of them knelt beside the wooden manger, and I could hear the mother praying. In a few minutes, they went on their way."

Later, another family came by and the children asked their mother, "What is that?" to which she coarsely replied, "I don't know."

Bonnie stepped forward and gently gave them an information sheet that described the significance of Christ's birth. That night they learned that Jesus came to give them eternal life, a gift their money could not buy.

Is There Room?

She wrapped him in clothes and placed him in a
manger, because there was no room for them in
the inn.
LUKE 2:7

In some places at Christmas, people place lanterns, or *farolitos*, along walls and paths or flat adobe roofs. Candles are set in sand inside paper bags and symbolize the journey of Joseph and Mary. These lanterns help the couple in their search for an empty room and reflect the starry light of Bethlehem that welcomed the Christ child's birth.

Rev. Douglas Showalter remembered the story of Mary and Joseph's search in a profound way one Christmas. In their white-steepled New England church, his parishioners always looked forward to the Christmas Eve service each year. In the dim auditorium, a group of young people fully presented the Nativity tableau.

This particular year, Rev. Showalter's church council realized Christmas Eve fell on the same night as the Alcoholics Anonymous large public meeting in their church fellowship hall. Would there be enough parking space? Would the AA group even attend, or would they want to spend the night with friends and family? Ultimately, the church leaders decided to let the AA group meet, regardless of the inconvenience.

The church parking lot overflowed as both AA and church members arrived. In the restroom that night, Rev. Showalter overheard a stranger—a young, sad-eyed teenage boy—talking to an older man: "I'm glad there's a meeting tonight. It's Christmas Eve, and I didn't have anywhere else to go." The older man from AA agreed.

Rev. Showalter watched the Nativity scene that night with a lump in his throat, grateful they had kept their "Inn" open to the ones who needed it.[13]

Our lives are like lanterns lighting the way to hope. When others come to us, looking for a safe place to shelter their hearts, will we cry "no room," or will we, like Rev. Showalter's church, keep our doors open to all who need the Savior's love?

Second Impressions

You are to judge your neighbor fairly.
LEVITICUS 19:15 NASB

Was that the doorbell? Peggy peered through a crack in the living room draperies. She hardly knew her new neighbors, but she could see that the lady from across the street stood impatiently on the front porch. Peggy barely had time to open the door before the neighbor blurted out, "Neighborhood caroling. Saturday night. Meet at our house—7:00 pm." Without giving Peggy a chance to reply, the neighbor hurried back across the street.

Though the neighborhood looks friendly with all of its Christmas decorations, the people sure aren't, thought Peggy. The elderly man next door only grumped at her whenever she said hello. And the weird couple behind her house kept a toilet on their front porch. Strange!

When Peggy heard the sounds of caroling that frosty Saturday evening, something prompted her to bundle herself into her coat. As the neighbors caroled from house to house, Peggy tagged along, singing and listening to conversations. What she heard surprised her. The "impatient" neighbor lady took care of a handicapped son who required round-the-clock supervision. The "grumpy" neighbor had a speech impediment that made his words come out in grunts and growls. The "weird" man with the toilet used his unusual porch decoration as a unique conversation starter to tell others about God's love. The more Peggy heard, the more she realized that her first impressions of her neighbors had been wrong.

Later, as the neighbors gathered around steaming mugs of cocoa, Peggy decided to make some "second" impressions. She smiled at the "impatient" neighbor and said, "Hi, I'm Peggy. Do you have a minute to talk?"

———————————————

Gifts for a Lifetime

Each of you should look not only to your own
interests, but also to the interests of others.
PHILIPPIANS 2:4

"Mom, can't we do something different for Christmas? We always give Daddy a tie, a shirt, or cologne. *Boooooring.* And when we're all finished unwrapping those *boooring* gifts, there's such a letdown. Do you have any ideas?"

One family struggled with that Christmas scenario and decided to tackle "something different." The adults of their family chose not to exchange gifts. Instead, on Christmas day they passed a brightly wrapped box to each adult. Inside the box, the adults had placed a certain amount of money — approximately what they would have spent for each other at Christmas. The total amount was impressive.

Soon after Christmas they discovered a need in their small town: members of their Special Olympics team needed uniforms. With their gift, they purchased shoes and full uniforms for two participants.

Others found equally satisfying ways to give unique gifts at Christmas. Carol sorted through her jewelry and mementos she'd collected during her husband's military tours. "With delight and tears," she said, "I gave my daughters thirty-year-old pearls from Japan, jade and sapphire rings from Hong Kong, a cameo from Italy, a piece of crystal from Ireland."

"These were gifts that meant more than money," she continued, "Family treasures that each had special meaning to my daughters."

One woman stood outside her friends' homes and sang Christmas carols off-key, while another baked loaves of bread from a one hundred-year-old recipe and delivered them, with her family, to friends and neighbors.

Mary chose to buy magazines from the month and year her friends and family members were born; another selected college courses to give away: business course, cooking course, golf lessons, piano lessons, computer course.[14]

There is one gift we can all offer others, regardless of how much we've deposited into our Christmas budget. It's called T-I-M-E.

It's Too Hard!

Rest in the Lord, and wait patiently for Him.
PSALM 37:7 NKJV

The three children stole silently down the stairs. In hushed whispers they reminded each other of the creaky board on the landing. They stayed carefully away from the window, lest the bright moonlight cast their shadows on the hallway below. In just a few more steps they would find out the secret.

They carefully placed their slippered feet on the carpeted treads to mask any sounds of movement. Yet a cry rang out, "Children, if you don't get back in bed, Christmas will never come!"

The three children wheeled around and scrambled back up the stairs to their bedroom.

"How did she know?" wailed one.

"You must have made a sound," growled another.

"We were as quiet as you," protested the third.

Mother's footsteps on the stairway silenced their quarreling. Her silhouetted form appeared in the doorway. Though the children could not see her face, her voice sounded like she was smiling as she said, "I know you're excited that tomorrow is Christmas, but you need to get some sleep."

"But, Mom," the oldest whined, "waiting is too hard. We've already waited all year for Christmas!"

Mother busily tucked the wanderers back into their beds. "Just wait a little longer," she replied. "Remember, God says waiting patiently is worth it."

Obediently, the three children snuggled into their beds. And Mother's words proved true to those three youngsters. Their patient waiting resulted in wonderful surprises at the bottom of the stairway on Christmas morning—surprises that would have been ruined by their sneaking and peeking. Truly God does bring good things to those who wait!

A Christmas Blessing

He gives you something you can then give
away . . . so that you can he generous in every
way, producing with us great praise to God.
2 CORINTHIANS 9:11 MSG

Glen patted the wallet in his back pocket. He had landed a job after school as grocery checker at Fergeson's Super Market and had just cashed his first paycheck. In two weeks, he would be able to make the down payment for that 1985 Chevrolet at Bud's used car lot. A bicycle was fine for kids. But Glen was tired of the guys teasing him at school.

Times were tough for Glen and his mom. His father, an alcoholic, died in a drunken brawl when Glen was only ten. His mom suffered with chronic asthma but ironed clothes to pay the bills. Glen delivered papers for several years to supplement their income, but this new job promised more: a future. The thought of managing his own store someday made Glen swell with pride.

Upon leaving, Glen heard a commotion in the checkout line. A shabbily dressed woman pleaded with the checker: "But I must feed my babies! I don't have enough money! It's almost Christmas!"

People grumbled in line. The checker looked angry.

Glen sighed deeply and walked over to the lady. "Excuse me," he said, pulling her away from prying eyes. Without hesitation, he reached into his pocket and placed the bills into her trembling hands. "Shh! Now go buy your groceries." Glen tore loose from the woman's grateful embrace and rode home.

A few days later, Glen found an envelope from Mr. Fergeson in his time card slot. Inside it read, "Promoted to assistant manager. I need people with unselfish hearts in my business. Merry Christmas!" In the envelope was a $200 advance.

Trouble knocks at every door. But we can always find someone who suffers more. In God's plan of economy, we are blessed so that we can bless others. In the process, He always meets our own needs.

A Pastor's Present

*I want you to have the good
that comes from giving.*
PHILIPPIANS 4:17 NCV

John had a problem. As a clergyman, he didn't make much money, his personal resources were limited, and his schedule was filled to overflowing. But Christmas was coming, and he had always sent a present to his nephews and nieces in Vermont. Unless a miracle happened, John would have to forego that custom.

Extra income to purchase gifts for his young relatives eluded him at every turn. John had tried to sell a few of his short stories and articles to make some extra money, but none of the publishers showed any interest. His paintings and drawings sat unsold in a local gallery. So John decided to make the children a gift. Even if the publishers didn't appreciate his writings, maybe his nephews and nieces would.

With pen in hand that autumn afternoon in 1857, John sat at his well-worn desk and prayed a simple prayer for God's help and direction. As he finished his prayer, John recalled the Bible passage that told of the kings who followed a star to See the Christ child in Bethlehem. And John Henry Hopkins began to write . . . "We three kings of Orient are. . . ."

Shortly after sending the poem to his young relatives, John added a compelling melody and offered the entire carol as a musical addition to the General Theological Seminary of New York's Christmas pageant that year. John's prayer for God's help was answered in a wonderful way. Since then, this pastor's gift has become a treasured Christmas classic, a story of hope that can guide us all to the perfect light of joyful giving.[15]

Where's the Christmas?

*Be imitators of God as dear children
and walk in love.*
EPHESIANS 5:1-2 NKJV

A young man won a trip to America. "I have heard so much about this celebration of Christmas in America. I cannot wait to see for myself just what is so special about it," he said to the friend who was seeing him off.

When the plane landed in a large metropolitan city, the man hailed a taxi. "I am here to see Christmas. Can you tell me what this Christmas is all about? Please take me to the places where I can find out more about it."

The taxi driver gave him some suggestions, including the place where he might stay, then dropped him off downtown. A few days later, the man flew home and his friend picked him up at the airport. "Well, how was it? What did you see?"

The man frowned.

"I do not know why this holiday is so special. I saw people pushing, shoving, and cursing in long lines in department stores, buying expensive gifts— with money that would have fed a family for a month. I saw selfish children yelling at their parents and other adults fighting over a strange-looking toy. At another store, I saw people buying cases of liquor. I watched them later as they swaggered from parties in a drunken stupor. Cars honked, racing through the streets, as if traveling to a fire. I heard music playing—something about joy and peace—but there is more peace in our own country than what I saw there. So I returned home. I do not understand what is so special about this Christmas holiday."

How difficult would it be for strangers to uncover the beauty of Christmas should they visit our homes or our cities? How long would they have to search before they discovered the true meaning of *peace, good will toward men*?

The King's Kids

Therefore the Lord Himself will give you a sign:
Behold, a virgin will be with child and bear a
son, and she will call His name Immanuel.
ISAIAH 7:14 NASB

Beautiful dark-eyed, dark-haired Dana tearfully related her painful experience of becoming pregnant out of wedlock. But her eyes brightened as she explained that while visiting the Crisis Pregnancy Center, a young woman had introduced her to Jesus Christ. Dana received His forgiveness and began a new life. Through hard times as a single mom with a baby girl, she knew that God loved her and would provide for her needs. Dana is now married to a fine Christian man, is actively involved in her church's intercessory prayer ministry, and takes every opportunity to share Christ with others.

The first seventeen verses of the book of Matthew list some of the women in Christ's lineage who had shady backgrounds. There was Rahab, the harlot; and Tamar, who tricked and seduced her father-in-law and had a child by him. Yet another, Bathsheba, had an adulterous relationship with King David. In spite of their failures and sins—and because of God's grace—these women were honored. God redeemed them, allowing them to be remembered as ancestors of Jesus.

The mystery of Christmas is a moment in time when the Incarnate defies human comprehension. Immanuel—God with us, in us, over us, through us. Just as God used all kinds of people to bring His Son into the world, we marvel at how today He works in a supernatural way through ordinary people—sinners—to accomplish His will. God's sovereignty can never be thwarted.

Oh, My Head!

*Let's go to Bethlehem and see this thing that has
happened, which the Lord has told us about.*
LUKE 2:15

Kristi's favorite part of Christmas was helping her
mother unpack the manger scene. Around the first of
November, Kristi and Mother cleared the top of the
piano to make room for the hand-carved holy family,
wise men, and townspeople figures which came with
interesting stories about their search for the Savior.

Each figure was lovingly removed from its original
box, marked with a detailed description.

"Hurry, Mom, hurry! Find my favorite man," said
Kristi.

Mother checked the remaining boxes and retrieved
the one marked "man with headache."

"Here he is, Kristi. Find him a spot to see Jesus."

"Okay, Mom, tell me again. Why does he have a headache?" Kristi never tires of hearing the same story again.

Each year the figures seem to come alive as Kristi's mother tells made-up stories about the hardships endured on the way to the manger.

Over his arm, Man with Headache carries a small food basket. Clutching his hat, he holds his right hand to his stomach. He holds his head with his left hand. Perhaps, he had worked hard in the few days before his journey. His wife and three small children are left behind. Along the way, the man has slept poorly, as this is his first lengthy journey away from his family. Because his children are young, Man with Headache had to find a willing friend to oversee his flock while he is gone. Despite the difficulties of the trip, the man's anticipation of seeing Jesus makes it all worthwhile.

This time of year is extremely busy. Don't let it overwhelm you, or you may find yourself with a headache! Let the anticipation of His coming make everything worthwhile.

Joy of Another Kind

He has sent me to bind up the brokenhearted.
ISAIAH 61:1

Dr. Norman Vincent Peale once shared an experience he had on Christmas Eve. As he left the house of friends after dinner that night, he noticed the house across the street. Two wreaths hung on the door —one a Christmas wreath, the other a funeral wreath. He asked his friends about the family living there, but they knew only bare facts: a nice family, three children —one who had died that morning.

Dr. Peale said he paced for a long time, trying to decide whether to intrude on this family's grief. But after all, this was Christmas Eve, and broken hearts might need a loving, caring touch. So he rang the doorbell. The husband was entertaining the two small children downstairs as they played beside the twinkling Christmas tree, determined to keep joy alive

126

this night. But tearfully, he asked Dr. Peale to speak to his wife.

In an upstairs room he found the young mother sitting beside her daughter's lifeless form. He heard no bitter words, no "Why, God?" Only "thank You's" to God for loaning her child to them for three years.

Dr. Peale said, "I thought of that other Baby born so long ago who in manhood spoke of the heavenly mansions in the Father's house beyond this life."[16] And that day the little girl had found a new home in those mansions.

The celebration of Christmas, in all of its joy and cheer, cannot remove the pain from hurting hearts.

But grateful hearts, bared before Him in honesty, can find the path to healing in the Child-man, Heaven's own gift, who wipes away all tears from our eyes and restores beauty from ashes.

Just One More

Cheerfully share your home
with those who need a meal.
1 PETER 4:9 TLB

The company Christmas party had always been held in the company dining room on the first Saturday of December. But this year the president suggested that each department celebrate Christmas in its own way. Within days, posters appeared advertising the upcoming departmental festivities. The art department invited its people to an impromptu Christmas picnic at a nearby church hall. The advertising department splurged on symphony tickets for interested departmental employees. The sales department advertised a potluck supper with a sign-up sheet and a map to the sales manager's home.

A week before the potluck supper, the sales manager began preparations for his departmental Christmas party. His living and dining room easily accommodated folding tables and chairs for the twenty of his employees who would be attending, so the manager thought his preparations were complete.

A phone call later that night increased the seating to twenty-one when he agreed that his secretary could bring her husband. After all, the man reasoned, what's the harm in just one more. But the twenty-one became twenty-six when other associates asked to bring family members too. Soon the twenty-six became thirty-eight, the thirty-eight became forty-two, and by the night of the party the guest list had grown to sixty-four! Rented folding tables and chairs filled the sales manager's home from the basement to the top floor. Despite the fact that there was always a waiting line at the bathroom, employees say that because the sales manager opened his home and his heart to "just one more," it was their best Christmas party ever![17]

The Song Heard 'Round the World

Shout for joy to the Lord, all the earth,
burst into jubilant song with music.
PSALM 98:4

A beautiful story from *Christmas in My Heart,* compiled by Dr. Joe Wheeler, tells about one doctor's agonizing choice between life and death. Dr. Frederic Loomis had to decide whether to allow a baby with a severely deformed leg to die during its birth. Why not let the breech birth take its course and end in death? Why contribute to someone's suffering when he could alleviate it so easily? Who would know anyway?

Ultimately, Dr. Loomis said no. He delivered the baby.

Seventeen years later at a Christmas party, the old physician listened as a beautiful young woman with a prosthesis played brilliantly on a harp. The girl's mother saw the doctor and identified the musician as her daughter—the one Dr. Loomis had delivered years ago as a baby.[18]

Another family was blessed by a baby, too, despite the odds. When Leslie Galey was four months pregnant, unborn baby Joel's x-rays revealed spina bifida. Doctors offered to terminate the pregnancy. But Leslie and her husband, Kevin, prayed fervently for a miracle, seeking other possibilities and opinions. About a month and a half before the baby's birth, surgeons lifted Leslie's uterus from her body, opened it, and closed the hole in the baby's back. On December 14, 1998, the Galeys witnessed the miraculous birthing cries of a 5.5-pound baby boy. It was music to their ears. At a year old, the baby continues to do well. The surgery worked.

Two thousand years ago, a young virgin could have faced a similar decision when an unexpected Baby threatened to turn her world upside down. Because she and her betrothed husband chose to obey and birth the Son of God, the most beautiful music ever written was heard around the world: an eternal song of joy.

And we're still singing it today.

———————————————

Wartime Christmas Gift

I will never desert you,
nor will I ever forsake you.
HEBREWS 13:5 NASB

With perspiration dripping from his face, the dejected young soldier trudged through deep sand toward the hooch (a tropical shelter) as memories of Christmases past raced through his mind. There in Cam Ranh Bay, South Vietnam, the Christmas of 1966 would certainly be different. No home-cooked meals, no family celebrations, no fireplace and hot chocolate, and no snuggling with his wife on a cold, wintry night. The officer missed his home. In fact, the emptiness left a crater-size ache in his stomach and loneliness so severe that he choked back tears.

Then from a distance he began to hear the sound of men singing. "Silent Night, Holy Night." Instinctively, he felt drawn toward the melody and followed it to a rustic makeshift chapel. When he stepped inside, he discovered men of all colors and religious persuasions sitting shoulder to shoulder, singing about Jesus' birth. He quietly scooted onto the bench at the back and added his quivering voice to theirs.

In a mysterious way, his emptiness gave way to an inner glow as he participated in the worship service and listened to the small voice within his heart that said, "I have something just for you." The soldier soon recognized and began to appreciate his gift: not one wrapped in colorful paper and ribbons, but a reassuring sense of God's presence and His provision of a spiritual family to offer encouragement and hope.

DEAR LORD,

Bless our men and women in uniform wherever they are serving. Help each to discover Your gift to them: an enduring promise of Your presence. Comfort them with Your love.

AMEN.

Give Your Best

*From everyone who has been given much, much
will be demanded; and from the one who has been
entrusted with much, much more will be asked.*
LUKE 12:48

Mrs. Gibson's kindergarten class filed onto the stage. This was the day they had all waited and practiced for. The children bounced with excitement, every boy and girl dressed in his or her Christmas best. The stage was a plethora of red, white, green, smiles, and wiggles!

The program progressed smoothly. Mrs. Gibson smiled at the children, and they smiled back. They seemed to remember every instruction she had given them before they left the room. Mrs. Gibson began to relax and enjoy the presentation.

Chris was one of the last children to speak and stepped proudly to the microphone. He took a deep breath and began. "The wise men brought their best gifts to Jesus. They brought Gold, Frankenstein, and Smurfs."

Chris got quite an ovation. He lingered for a moment behind the microphone, chest thrust out, all smiles. He had done his best.

That is all any of us can do. God gave His very best gift to us. When we bring our gifts to Jesus, they don't have to be perfect. They just need to be our best, given from a heart of love.

Give of your best to the Master,
Naught else is worthy His love;
He gave Himself for your ransom,
Gave up His glory above;
Laid down His life without murmur,
You from sin's ruin to save;
Give Him your heart's adoration,
Give Him the best that you have.
HOWARD B. GROSE

Still Giving and Giving and Giving

Each man should give what he has decided in his heart to give, not reluctantly or under compulsion, for God loves a cheerful giver.
2 CORINTHIANS 9:7

Some people think retirement is a time for donning shorts and beanie hats, and chasing white balls in the hot sun all day. Not so with Robert Fairchild of Tulsa, Oklahoma. At the age of eighty eight, Robert is "a little like the battery-powered bunny in the television commercials: He just keeps going and going and going — and giving and giving and giving."

A typical December day finds Robert smoking turkeys for a big Christmas dinner at a recreation center — after delivering Meals on Wheels in a cold, misty rain. "Volunteering in my community," Robert says, "is a very, very important part of my life. I'm glad to do it. I wish there was more I could do, because there are a lot of things that need to be done."

Robert also works with young people at the YMCA, mentoring middle school students, and tutoring elementary school children. And if that isn't enough, he also teaches adults to read through a local literacy program.

In 1992, Dan Rabovsky, the director of Meals on Wheels, said Mr. Fairchild "has the spirit of a teenager. Robert is a wonderful person. He is willing, literally, to give you the shirt off his back."

Some people wait for a divine invitation to give a helping hand. But Robert Fairchild already knows that giving is God's idea. "When we volunteer," he says, "we serve God."[19]

If each person would volunteer only one hour a day to benefit someone else, we could keep the Christmas spirit alive—all year long.

"Go break to the needy sweet charity's bread;
for giving is living," the angel said.
"And must I be giving again and again?"
My peevish and pitiless answer ran.
"Oh no," said the angel, piercing me through,
"Just give till the Master stops giving to you. "
AUTHOR UNKNOWN

Modern Magi

And do not forget to do good and to share with
others, for with such sacrifices God is pleased.
HEBREWS 13:16

Some might think Rebecca Borkovec could easily play a child's version of the wife in the beloved Christmas story *The Gift of the Magi*. This eight-year-old third grader of Greendale, Wisconsin, heard about the Locks of Love organization on a television commercial and decided to let her hair hang down for love — and a wig charity.

For two and a half years Rebecca grew long, beautiful locks. At times, her hair was a real drag — literally. When she was swimming or shampooing, her hair would pull her head down in water. Gymnastics brought problems too. Drying time seemed endless. But Rebecca kept her goal in sight. One day her hair would make a wonderful Christmas present for a child who had lost hair during chemotherapy.

Rebecca's mother encouraged her, took time to braid her hair, and kept fixing it in creative ways. And Rebecca reminded her mom often, "We have to get it trimmed, so it will look nice for someone."

On February 9, 2000, Rebecca settled into a chair at Barbara's TLC hair salon and signaled Barbara to start cutting. Was Rebecca sad to see her locks fall? She just sat there smiling. Why? "Because then the next time I went into the water, my head wouldn't be drooping down, and I was smiling because I was going to help people."

But Rebecca didn't stop there. "I'm going to do it again," she promised, "so I can help them again." It will probably take about three years.[20]

Most people give, if their money is headed toward research or a tax write-off, and if the sacrifice is not too great or time-consuming. Rebecca's gift brought her no tangible returns, only the sheer joy of knowing she gave a headful of love to someone in need.

———————————————

Who's on Top?

If you want to be right at the top,
you must serve like a slave.
MATTHEW 20:27 TLB

———————————

The church youth group had worked hard on their float for the Christmas parade. Constructing the three-tiered chicken wire hillside and Nativity scene had been difficult. The teens worked after school and on weekends, cutting wooden supports, stretching canvas over chicken wire forms, painting lifelike rock formations and ground covers. The float was almost complete, but there was still one major decision to make.

"You should be the angel on the top of the float, Susan," announced Kelly, "After all, we've built this float in your grandfather's barn, and it is the best spot on the float. You'd get to see everything."

"You're right, Kelly," said the youth pastor. "Susan's grandfather has been generous to let us use his barn. But there are other people who have helped with this project, too. Steve's dad gave us the lumber. Kelly's folks paid for the canvas. Tom's mother showed us how to paint everything. And don't forget Alicia. She's the newest member of our group, but she hand-hammered the skirting around the float all by herself. Why don't we take a moment and vote on place assignments?"

When the votes were tallied, Susan had been chosen to play Mary, Tom would fill in as Joseph, and Alicia would be the angel at the top of the float. As Susan gave Alicia a hug, Tom quipped, "Hooray for Alicia—a living example of someone who started at the bottom and made it to the top! Now let's get a picture of this chicken wire creation. Everybody . . . hold it . . . and smile!"

A Pauper's Birth

This will be a sign to you: you will find a baby
wrapped in clothes and lying in a manger.
LUKE 2:12

In his book *When Iron Gates Yield*, a British missionary to Tibet tells of a Christmas during the three years he was held captive by the Chinese Communists. He spent a long, tiring day crossing a mountain pass, then stumbled down the other side in heavy winds. Finally his captors brought him to some small huts. A Tibetan landlord had thoroughly cleaned an upstairs room for the missionary-prisoner. The missionary ate dinner and was then ordered to feed the horses downstairs in the dark. He climbed down the notched tree trunk to the bottom floor where his captives kept the stabled animals.

The missionary describes his feelings as he entered the stable in the pitch-black darkness:

My boots squished in the manure and straw on the floor and the fetid smell of the animals was nauseating. I felt my way amongst the mules and horses, expecting to be kicked any moment.

What a place, *I thought. Then as I continued to grope my way in the darkness towards the gray, it suddenly flashed into my mind.* What's today? *I thought for a moment. In the traveling, the days had become a little muddled in my mind.*

It's Christmas Eve. *I stood suddenly still in that oriental manger. To think that my Savior was born in a place like this. To think that He came all the way from heaven to some wretched, eastern stable, and what is more, to think that He came for me.*[21]

We often glorify the beauty of Christ's birth at Christmas, forgetting that the Son of God entered life with a pauper's beginnings. Yet what a wonder to realize anew—that He did it for me—and for you.

———————————————

Is That a Whale on the Ice?

Then was our mouth filled with laughter,
and our tongue with singing.
P S A L M   1 2 6 : 2   K J V

It was just a few days before Christmas, and Davids parents, brother, and sister were visiting from Texas for the holidays. David and his wife, Gail, lived in a small town in the mountains. Following a wonderful breakfast and a short drive, the brave-hearted (and foolish) attempted to ride a toboggan down the hills for a couple of hours.

After the toboggan rides, everyone headed for a frozen pond in an adjacent meadow and donned ice skates. What an experience — skating outdoors on a pond! Gail prepared hot chocolate by the fire and laid out the picnic lunch. The sky was so blue it hurt her eyes, and the crackle of the fire at the edge of the frozen pond merged with the sounds of laughter from the skaters to lend a "Norman Rockwell" quality to the day.

A few weeks later, the family was reliving the experience by looking at colored slides. One frame showed the frozen pond with a dark-colored mound rising in the center.

"What is that?" someone asked.

After much discussion, they finally figured it out.

"That's Dad!"

This was true. The dark mound was David's father, who had slipped down and was just lying still, resting on the ice. Then the jokes began, culminating with a laughing proclamation: "You know that really looks kind of like a beached whale on the ice." Much laughter and mock anger followed, and the joy of family love filled the room.

Holidays can be that way when families commit themselves to loving relationships. There is a simple joy in just being together during the special times of the year.

Hope Is Alive

The Word became flesh and made his dwelling
among us. We have seen his glory, the glory of
the One and Only, who came from the Father,
full of grace and truth.
J O H N 1 : 1 4

A clergyman fell asleep in his study on Christmas morn and dreamed about a world where Christ had never been born. As he dreamed, he walked through his own home but saw no stockings hung by the chimney. No Christmas wreaths adorned the walls. No tree stood shining with ornaments. As he walked into the street he searched for a church spire pointing to heaven, but found none. He returned to his house and entered the library where he looked for a book to encourage his faith. The books about his Savior were gone.

A messenger rang his doorbell and asked him to visit a dying woman. The minister grabbed his Bible and hastened to the woman's house. He tried to comfort her, but when he opened his Bible, he discovered the verses ended with Malachi and omitted the New Testament. Realizing he could offer no hope, he wept with the woman in despair.

Two days later at the woman's funeral, he stood silently beside the woman's coffin as others filed by. He could offer no consolation there or at the graveside. Where was the hope of the resurrection? The anticipation of heaven? He felt swallowed up in the familiar words, "ashes to ashes, and dust to dust."

The clergyman woke up sobbing, realizing the horror of his dream. Suddenly he heard the beautiful sound of a choir rehearsing in his church next door. He listened, paralyzed as the real truth dawned. Christ had come! He joined the choir's praises in the carol, *O Come, All Ye Faithful.*[22]

We can only imagine what our world would be like if Christ had not come. The good news is Christ was born; hope does exist, and inner peace is possible through God's heaven-sent gift. Isn't that what Christmas is all about?

––––––––––––––––––

A Cup of Love

*In everything, set them an example
by doing what is good.*
TITUS 2:7

The first cup and saucer came unannounced at Christmastime. The package had no markings or return address, but inside the cup was a note that read, "Enjoy a cup of God's love." Puzzled by this anonymous gift, Rose inquired about who could have sent it. But no one seemed to know.

The following Christmas another cup and saucer arrived in the same manner. And this process was repeated every Christmas for twelve years. A special shelf in the dining room held the twelve beautiful china cups and their matching saucers.

But on the thirteenth year, a smaller package came that explained the mystery. A letter inside told about a woman in the community who had befriended a woman named Mrs. Martin and given her a china cup and saucer to use for her morning coffee. Mrs. Martin was so touched by the simple gesture that she decided to share the kindness with someone else. But rather then limit her gift to a single act, Mrs. Martin instructed her lawyer to send cups and saucers to three women every year at Christmas, anonymously, until her death. This year there would be no cup and saucer because Mrs. Martin had died in early November.

Rose's gaze rested on her beautiful collection. Twelve years ago there had been no cups, no saucers, no reminders of God's love. Now there were so many beautiful memories because of Mrs. Martin's kindness.

Rose shook herself from her reverie and announced aloud, "It's almost Christmas, and someone needs a cup of God's love this year. Now where can I buy a cup and saucer?"

Love in the Straw

The King will reply, ". . . whatever you did for
one of the least of these brothers of mine, you did
for me."
MATTHEW 25:40

Niki Anderson probably faced the same dilemma that many parents do: how do you teach children to serve Christ by serving one another? She began a tradition at Christmas to show her children how, using the creche as an object lesson.

Piece by piece they unwrapped the figures of their Nativity set—all but Baby Jesus. Niki suggested they wait until Christmas Eve to put Him in the manger—and pretend that they were waiting for Jesus to be born. She then took straw from the crib and laid it in a pile outside the creche. When anyone did a kind deed for a member of the family, they took a piece of straw and put it in Jesus' crib.

Her children loved the idea. Each one began to outdo the other in performing good deeds, so they could fill up Jesus' crib with straw.

On Christmas Eve the family completed the creche by placing Baby Jesus in the manger. It was time for Him to be born!

Something else was born that night in the hearts of Niki's family. In succeeding days as one of her children would do a good deed, she'd hear, "I put straw in the crib, didn't I, Mom?"[23]

When Christ is truly born in our hearts, we will discover ways to celebrate Christmas all year long. We can then mirror Jesus as we go about doing good. What we do for others not only brings straws of comfort and joy to them, but a haystack of love for the Lord Himself.

———————————

The New Bike

If ye then, being evil, know how to give good
gifts unto your children, how much more shall
your Father which is in heaven give good things
to them that ask him?
MATTHEW 7:11 KJV

Stephen knew that although he would love to have a new bike, it probably just wasn't in the works this year. He remembered when he received his very first bicycle. It was bright red and perfect. He didn't know it at the time, but his father had taken an old bicycle and fixed it up to look new. To Stephen, it was beautiful, and he loved it. But now he was older and wanted a new Mattel Silver Stallion.

That same year, Stephen and the members of his Royal Rangers scouting troop had just completed refinishing a number of old bicycles for children in an orphanage. They had sanded the old bicycle frames, carefully removing any rust, smoothing the finish, and repainting them. Next they put on new seats, handlebars with colorful streamers, and inner tubes and tires. The remodeled bikes looked new, and the kids at the home were so excited when they received them.

On Christmas Eve, the family enjoyed a sumptuous dinner and opened nearly all the presents. Stephen was trying hard to hide his disappointment, for there was no bicycle under the tree for him. Then Stephen's mom and dad called him to look in the garage. And when he did, he saw the bicycle he had wanted so much. Somehow, someway his parents had found a means to give him "the bike"!

Parents are like that at Christmas—no sacrifice is too great when they want to give to their children. God is like that too, joyfully waiting until the moment we unwrap His gifts to us.

_____

What Can I Give?

And they did not do as we expected, but they
gave themselves first to the Lord and then to us
in keeping with God's will.
2 CORINTHIANS 8:5

Six-year-old Tracy listened to his mom read the last page of one of his favorite Christmas stories. For several years now during the holidays, Tracy and his mom would grab a blanket and a cup of hot chocolate and sit by the fire to read *The Littlest Angel.*

"I'm a lot like that littlest angel," Tracy finally spoke.

"What do you mean?"

"Well, the angel didn't have any expensive gifts to give to Jesus. Neither do I. At least he brought the Baby Jesus some beautiful things from his own 'treasure' collection—things that didn't cost much. But Mom, if Christmas is Jesus' birthday, what gift can I give to Jesus? I don't even have any 'collections' or treasures. I gave Sandy all the stuff out of my junk drawer last week. And Jesus sure doesn't need any of my toys. He's all grown up now."

"You could bake Jesus a cake. And we could wish Him happy birthday."

"Lots of people do that, Mom. I want to give Him something really — special."

The days grew closer to Christmas, and Tracy still had no ideas. Then on Christmas Eve morning, he woke up smiling. That night he had placed a small gift-wrapped box beside the Nativity set on his mantel.

On Christmas morning, Tracy asked his mom to open the box. There inside lay a piece of paper on which Tracy had colorfully written, "MYSELF"

Isn't that really what Jesus wants?

What gift have I for the Christ Child?
What token can I bring?
What offering of gratitude
Can I lay before the King?
A King deserves a royal prize,
Beyond all earthly measure.
I'll give my heart, and nothing less —
The highest of my treasure.

REBECCA BARLOW JORDAN[24]

Love in Action

Dear friends, since God so loved us,
we also ought to love one another.
1 JOHN 4:11

In his book *You Can Win with Love,* Dale Galloway relates a story about his mother, who lived in Ohio. She loved to visit the rest homes in her town and cheer the shut-ins who lived there. The personnel asked Dale's mom to consistently visit one lady named Sally. The woman had some mental problems, and for the first few visits told Dale's mom she didn't want to see her — or anyone.

But Dale's mom, believing this was God's ministry for her, determined to make friends with the woman. She talked to Sally's sister and discovered Sally liked bananas. The next time she visited Sally, Dale's mom brought her a banana.

Week by week, his mom took Sally a banana or something good to eat. Little by little, Sally began to respond. She even let his mom hug her. One day, Dale's mom told her about Jesus' love for her, and Sally responded eagerly.

Weeks later, Dale's mom asked Sally if she loved Jesus. Dale wrote, "This forgotten woman, with a mental condition, answered, 'I love Him a whole lot more since you've been coming to see me.'"[25]

Perhaps Dale's mom had discovered a secret about love: "Nobody will know what you mean by saying that 'God is love' unless you act it as well."[26]

Laney learned that secret too. Concerned that she had no ministry, this new believer decided there were many "Sallys" who needed love. She and her two small preschoolers began visiting the local nursing homes once a week. Few people knew about Laney's ministry, and even fewer knew that for many years, she had suffered from chronic panic attacks—caused by a fear of public places.

A little love truly goes a long way. God knew that too. That's why He put Christmas in our hearts.

———————————————

Let Your Light Shine

The Lord is God,
and he has made his light shine upon us.
PSALM 118:27

Many neighborhoods celebrate the Christmas season with a Festival of Lights. They may set aside an evening for placing candles along walkways, following the ancient fashion of luminaries. Some places offer a prize to the homeowner who decorates with the most colorfully lit Christmas display. Tall buildings may be topped with crosses or stars. Skyscrapers sometimes sport outlines of wreaths or Christmas trees. City streetlights often wear garlands of tinsel and twinkling lights, too.

In addition, Christmas lights can be seen off in the distance — a home with its eaves outlined in a soft glow, a farmer's tractor or a transport truck bedecked with lights that catch a traveler's eye, or a spotlight trained on a quiet Nativity scene beside a country church. The lights of Christmas are a true feast for the eyes.

Yet some of the most beautiful lights of Christmas are the simple candles that shine in the windows of the houses we pass on our way home from running errands or commuting from work each night. The welcoming glow of those incandescent candles can slow us down, calm our hurried rushing, and remind us of God's gift to us that first Christmas. God's Son came to be a Light in our dark world. God's Son was one Candle, shining in the darkness — one Savior, bringing hope to humanity.

This season, let's let each sparkling Christmas light remind us of God's great gift to us, and let's share His light and love with others, too.

Laughing All the Way

A cheerful heart is good medicine.
P R O V E R B S   1 7 : 2 2

Ruth Bell Graham shares the story of one year when her family decided to have a Christmas "more spiritual and less commercial than usual."

She described her living room in typical American fashion: sparkling tree, stockings bulging from the mantel over the fireplace, and gifts—spreading "halfway across the living room floor."

Ruth's married children and their families had joined the celebration, and before opening gifts, they chose to have breakfast together: rolls, juice, coffee, and traditional oyster stew, "for those who liked it." This would allow the lady helping them to continue with her own Christmas dinner preparations. So the smaller children waited.

Then Ruth's husband, Billy, assuring them he would not take long, opened his Bible and shared devotions before they opened their gifts and stockings. Prayers followed. And the children waited, restless to continue.

But Ruth said the straw that broke the camel's back came when Anne asked the children to file slowly down the two steps into the living room so that she could get moving pictures of them as they entered the living room.

"Stephan Nelson, age five, was standing beside me, his back turned and his arms folded across his chest. Giving a deep sigh of disgust, he exclaimed under his breath, 'Bethlehem was never as miserable as this!'"[27]

Charles Dickens said, "It is good to be children sometimes, and never better than at Christmas, when its mighty Founder was a child Himself."

Besides reducing the stress of hectic holidays with their innocent wonder, children also keep us laughing all the way.

The Gift of Childhood

The child is not dead but asleep.
MARK 5:39

———————————

In his book *All I Really Need to Know I Learned in Kindergarten* Robert Fulghum offers a humorous yet poignant spin on Christmas gift-giving.

Fulghum says, "God cared enough to send the very best. On more than one occasion. And the Wise Men did not come bearing tacky knickknacks. . . . And the Angels came bringing Good News, which was not about a half-price sale."

And then Fulghum tells what he really wishes someone would give him for Christmas, something he's known since he was forty years old. Not socks. Not ties. Not paperweights or dust-catchers.

In his own words, Fulghum says:

It's delight and simplicity that I want.
Foolishness and fantasy and noise.

Angels and miracles and wonder
and innocence and magic. . . .
I want to be five years old again for an hour.
I want to laugh a lot and cry a lot.
I want to be picked up
and rocked to sleep in someone's arms,
and carried up to bed just one more time.
I know what I really want for Christmas.
I want my childhood back.

Fulghum agrees that this wish doesn't make sense. But Christmas, he says, is not about sense. "It is about a child, of long ago and far away, and it is about the child of now. In you and me. Waiting behind the door of our hearts for something wonderful to happen. . . . A child who does not need or want or understand gifts of socks or potholders."[28]

Fulghum also says nobody can give him that childhood back. But at Christmas, that's exactly what God did. Through Jesus, he awakened the sleeping child within us so we could see and experience life through the eyes of heaven's own Babe.

Putting the Pieces Together

God works in all of us in everything we do.
1 CORINTHIANS 12:6 NCV

Glaring the early 1860s, Philadelphia clergyman Phillips Brooks took a trip to the Holy Land. His visit gave him the opportunity to see firsthand some of the places he spoke about in his Sunday sermons. Years later, as Brooks sat in his office before he began preparations for his Advent series of sermons, something prompted him to pen several verses about his recollections of that trip.

At the same time Lewis Redner, a real estate agent and part-time organist for Rev. Brooks' church, struggled to put together the final pieces for an upcoming Sunday school Christmas program. Though he had found several new songs for the program, Redner felt that there was still something missing. Yet the night before the program, Redner went to sleep with a deep assurance that all would be well. Just as the first light of dawn split the sky, Redner awoke with a melody playing in his head. He jotted the notes down as quickly as he could and hurried to the pastor's home to play the piece for Rev. Brooks.

As the pastor heard the simple tune, he rushed into his office and reappeared moments later, carrying the poem he had penned only a few days ago. When the men compared the words of Brooks' poem with Redner's melody, both were amazed. The two were a perfect match. There was little doubt in either man's mind that God had orchestrated the entire composition. Two men, willing to follow God's tug on their hearts, contributed their small gifts to God's greater one, and "O Little Town of Bethlehem" was born.[29]

———————————————

Keep Shining

*And we, who with unveiled faces all reflect the
Lord's glory, are being transformed into his
likeness with ever-increasing glory, which comes
from the Lord.*
2 CORINTHIANS 3:18

The infamous Christmas school play is approaching. The teacher makes the announcement. The children's voices rise in excitement as they listen to the parts needed. Who will they portray? A humble donkey? A very handsome wise man? A faithful shepherd? One-of the dazzling angels, perhaps? A humpbacked camel? Woolly sheep? Who will be chosen to play the most favored parts in the Nativity — Mary and Joseph?

At home, parents pray for wisdom to help their children see that every part is important—and to comfort the ones who may not be chosen this time. The teacher assures that everyone will participate, but some will work on stage sets, painting and hammering. Others will be assigned technical parts such as lighting and sound effects.

Sue Monk Kidd may have experienced some of those parental emotions as she waited to see which part her small daughter would play. The answer: a Bethlehem star. What on earth would she do as a star?

In her own words Sue describes the scene after her daughter's first play rehearsal:

"She burst through the door with her costume, a five-pointed star lined in shiny gold tinsel designed to drape over her like a sandwich board. 'What exactly will you be doing in the play?' I asked her.

"'I just stand there and shine,' she told me."[30]

Sue says some of us choose the destiny of the tinsel star all our lives, pouring ourselves into a long line of praiseworthy accomplishments. Our aim is to do everything with dazzle and win accolades.

On the other hand, perhaps it's not such a bad role to play in life after all—to just "stand there and shine" —if we truly are reflecting not our own light, but the greatest Star of all.

——————————————

It's about Joy

I have told you this so that my joy may be in you
and that your joy may be complete.
JOHN 15:11

Clayton had searched a long time for joy. After all, joy *is* what Christmas is all about, isn't it? But in church after church, Clayton and his family found no room for joy—no place of acceptance for those with physical limitations like Clayton's. Denise Briley, his mother, found that other churches offered a place for handicapped children but separate from the nursery. And the children there felt no challenge. They were bored.

But that was before JOY was born at Graceview Baptist Church in Tomball, Texas. Graceview was the only church to contact Denise's family, asking how they could help with Clayton. At first, twelve-year-old Clayton, who suffered with congenital cytomegalo virus—causing severe cerebral palsy and vision impairment—stayed with the kindergarten class.

Then one night Denise had a dream where she saw Clayton smiling, accepted, and making friends of his own with other children. She discussed her idea with two church staff members. The pastor dubbed the new ministry, "JOY"—Jesus' Opportunity for You—and challenged his congregation to make a difference by reaching out to those with special needs.

Volunteers came—five at first, along with their sole pupil, Clayton. Gradually, the class increased to twenty students, ranging in age from five to fifty.

One seventy-year-old woman found such joy in this ministry that she painted a picture and called it "Joy in the Morning." In the painting she pictured children free of handicaps, sitting in Jesus' arms in heaven.

JOY spread to three classes, including one for those who live in their homes or in group homes, support groups, quarterly volunteer training sessions, and a parents' night out.[31]

JOY—an infectious condition easily caught. First conceived in God's mind and heart, then born in a lowly manger two thousand years ago.

The rest is history.

———————————————

Mama's Prayers

If you believe, you will get any thing
you ask for in prayer.
MATTHEW 21:22 NCV

It didn't look like Christmas. It didn't even feel like Christmas. It was too green, too warm, too un-Christmasy that year in the Catskill Mountains. Mountains mean snow in December. But this year, record temperatures kept the grass green. Ski resorts were hanging laundry on the rope tow lines. The weathermen predicted an usually warm and green Christmas day. Irving Berlin's "White Christmas" would remain a dream for the residents of the Catskill region, the television newsmen insisted.

"You don't know Mama," Martha muttered to the television as the family came trooping home from the grocery store.

When the last bag of goodies for the family's Christmas feast had been unloaded, Martha gave her siblings the dire news — no snow for Christmas.

"But," she continued, "Mama has been praying."

"Oh, boy," chirped the youngest. "I'm going to get my sled."

"Yeah!" chimed another, "Have you seen my snow pants?"

The youngsters chased one another down the hall searching for their snow gear. And Martha chuckled. Mama prayed for snow on Christmas only when Aunt Ellie came home. Aunt Ellie was a missionary in Africa. But whenever she came home at Christmastime, Mama asked God for the one thing her sister could never have in equatorial Africa — snow.

When the family went to bed on Christmas Eve, the weathermen still predicted a green Christmas. But Martha's family was prepared for a miracle, because Mama had been praying. On Christmas morning God answered Mama's prayer with a glistening snowfall that blanketed everything. The weathermen never could explain where all the snow came from, but then again, they never asked Mama!

———————————————

Brown Cups

My cup runneth over. Surely goodness
and mercy shall follow me all the days of my life.
P S A L M   2 3 : 5 - 6   K J V

———————————

They were probably the ugliest coffee cups Jimmy could have chosen. He was ten years old and had used his own money to buy his mom's Christmas present—a set of eight thick, brown ceramic coffee cups.

Throughout the summer and fall, Jimmy had searched the neighborhood roadsides for abandoned soft-drink bottles that he could return to the local convenience store for the deposit on them—regular size brought three cents; the larger ones brought five cents. He had also saved money from mowing lawns. Now, for the first time in his life he was giving his mom and dad Christmas gifts that he paid for with money he alone had earned.

It felt really, really neat.

It felt even better when Mom opened the present, smiled, hugged him, and told him they were just what she wanted.

It feels best, though, when he sits at the table with her today (over thirty years later) and drinks a cup of coffee from one of these same brown cups. The atmosphere at the table is always one of goodness and mercy as Jimmy is blessed with a special relationship with his parents. They are the ones whose love and support fill his "cup" to overflowing. Through their love, Jimmy knows God's love firsthand.

Who would have ever thought that a set of thick, brown ceramic coffee cups given as a Christmas gift so long ago could contain so many memories and flow with such warmth and love for so many years? Only God.

The Shoebox

A scroll of remembrance was written in his
presence concerning those who feared the Lord.
M A L A C H I   3 : 1 6

God may have a "scroll of remembrance," but this couple has a shoebox. Faded snapshots fill the box and record the passage of time, the celebrations, the gifts, and the visits spent with family. They smile at faded photos of their two-year-old astride a yellow, four-wheeled, scoot-along pony, grinning wildly in front of the Christmas tree. At three years old, she treasures her shiny tricycle delivered one Christmas morning. A few years later the snapshots reveal the excitement and glee as their daughter perches on a two-wheeler with butterfly handlebars, a banana seat, and training wheels.

Another series of photos come into focus. A Christmas tree glows softly beside the bay window, presents scattered underneath its full branches. Tucked behind the tree, almost hidden from view, is a racing bike, royal blue with handbrakes. And there she is, eyes alight with happiness, expertly maneuvering this newest treasure through the house and back alongside the Christmas tree.

Still shimmering with glossy newness, the next set of candid shots showcases a small box tucked under the Christmas tree. The box opens to reveal her very own set of car keys for the family car. Her smile lights up the room.

As the couple places the photos back in their "shoebox of remembrance," they say a prayer of thanks for God's goodness. They seal the lid with a kiss and promise to take time during the busy Christmas season next year to hold time between their fingers and remember again.

Passing the Baton

How beautiful are the feet of those
who bring good news!
R O M A N S   1 0 : 1 5

———————————————

Dr. Peggy Rummel of Colquitt, Georgia, had a late Christmas wish. When doctors told her in January that liver cancer would probably kill her in eight weeks, she spent time creating memories for her family. For others who knew her well in the one- stoplight town of southwestern Georgia, the forty-three-year-old doctor wanted more than nostalgia.

Dr. Rummel faced her share of difficulties through the years: Ulcerative colitis resulted in a colectomy and ileostomy fourteen years before — then the removal of her gall bladder. Rummel also suffered with brittle diabetes, autoimmune dysfunction, and Graves disease. A rose garden fungus produced an abscess in her head. Still, family and friends said she bore it all with the same sense of humor that got her through her medical residency.

Her wish? To find a replacement for herself after she died—a new doctor for the small Georgia town of Colquitt. But filling the shoes of someone who would sit through eight hours of labor with a maternity patient, work the emergency room at all hours, help raise eight foster children besides her own family, and help keep the local hospital afloat in a crisis would not be easy.

Dr. Rummel's tireless search on the internet paid off, and she lived to see her wish come true. Peggy Rummel surpassed her doctor's prognosis by several months. A week before she died, on Friday, May 7, 1999, Dr. Simon, who had completed his residency in Columbus, agreed to take over the practice. And keeping medicine in the family was Rummels own son, a pre-med major at Georgia Southwestern University.[32]

Peace on earth and spiritual healing in the hearts of every receptive person depend to a large degree on those who would hand the "baton" to someone else and keep spreading the good news of Christmas.

Who is replacing you?

Do All the Good You Can

Love your enemies, do good to them.
LUKE 6:35

One Christmas years ago, some townspeople wanted to share God's love in a practical way. They planted a vegetable garden beside the railroad tracks in a deserted area outside of town. The townspeople hoed, planted, and watered the garden until it produced a great harvest.

With knowing smiles, they laid down their tools in the garden and went about their business, content to let nature take its course.

Over the next year, they planted nothing else and never picked a vegetable. But the garden grew and grew and grew, yet vegetables seldom rotted in the garden. Weeds were scarce, and the garden always seemed to have that "specially tended to" look.

Was it a miracle? Perhaps. An untold number of homeless hobos riding the railroads—perhaps dozens, perhaps hundreds—helped themselves to the crop and often spent many hours looking after the garden.

For the hobos, Christmas happened year-round when they could always count on the blessings of good food—especially tasty as the fruit of their hard labors.

All around us are "hungry hobos" who need to know someone cares. Look for practical ways to share the love of Jesus with anyone who needs Him. You may be surprised by the harvest you reap.

A Picture of Hope

And hope does not disappoint us, because God
has poured out his love into our hearts by the
Holy Spirit, whom he has given us.
ROMANS 5:5

Norman Vincent Peale recalled a special evening years ago on Christmas Eve. His church was distributing large Christmas baskets to less fortunate families in the neighborhood. He offered to deliver the last basket himself.

He found the shack at the back of some other rundown buildings. A tired, overworked young woman who had been washing clothes in an old-fashioned tub, greeted him at the door. Dr. Peale glanced over at the worn couch, where he saw the woman's husband, who had obviously been drinking heavily.

The woman did not apologize. Instead, she defended him, calling him "a wonderful man" with just that one weakness. Other words followed, expressing her positive belief in her husband's overcoming future.

On the wall hung two paintings, their quality seemingly out of place with the rest of the shabby surroundings. The wife explained that the pictures were her husband's parents, a wonderful couple who represented hope to the young man.

Dr. Peale gave them the basket, but his story did not end there. He again visited them on Christmas day. The next week he saw the couple at church. Week after week they continued to come. On a bright July day they moved into a small, modest home, and Dr. Peale visited them again, where he saw the two paintings again hanging on the wall. As Dr. Peale left, the young man said cheerfully, "Merry Christmas!"

"Why not?" wrote Dr. Peale. "It was on Christmas that life began to be merry for this nice family."[33]

A thin thread of hope may be the only connection between the living and the dead for some—even for our own children and loved ones. An encouraging word, a caring deed, a constant belief in God's power to change can weave that thread into a life-saving rope of victorious joy.

_____

The Gift of Forgiveness

For God did not send his Son into the world to condemn the world, but to save the world through him.

JOHN 3:17

In his *Moments Together for Couples* devotions, Dennis Rainey shares a humorous Christmas incident about him and his wife, Barbara. One Christmas, Dennis was trying to place his beautiful seven-foot Scotch pine Christmas tree into a tiny stand. He whittled down the large trunk, but then the tree was too short to reach the bottom of the stand.

Barbara suggested he nail on an extension to the trunk of the tree. So he did. But with two blows of his hammer, both nails bent at a sharp angle to the one-inch block of wood. Muttering to himself that "Christmas trees must be a pagan ritual after all," Dennis tried again. And again. And again. Rainey says,

"Do you believe in demon-possessed Christmas trees?"
The following account relates his exasperation:

> *I threw the tree, flying needles and all, into the trunk of the car with the intent of taking this stupid, pagan, petrified thing back where I bought it. And then I looked at my horrified son, five-year-old Benjamin, who witnessed this display and probably thought that Christmas was about to be canceled. Just this once I should have taken W. C. Field's advice: "If at first you don't succeed, then quit! There's no use being a stupid fool about it!"*[34]

As Dennis Rainey pointed out, failure is a part of every life and every family. But one of the inherent Christmas truths is that God loves us—even in our failures. In fact, our failure is what prompted God to fill an earthly manger with an offering of forgiveness and love.

Two thousand years later, His offer still holds.

The Best Christmas Gift

It is more blessed to give than to receive.
A C T S 2 0 : 3 5

Exhausted from stretching the budget, Judy returned home from the grocery store in tears one day. She wanted to buy the perfect Christmas gift for her husband. However, with a near zero checkbook balance, Judy resigned herself to the inevitable and tried to be optimistic. *We can always exchange hugs,* she thought.

That night at the dinner table, the subject of finances rose as a hot topic. After a few minutes of emotional discussion, their three-year-old daughter blurted out, "If you want to give money, give it to the missionaries."

The couple looked at their daughter and then at each other with a *Huh?* kind of stare. Her comment made no sense at the moment, but they enjoyed a good laugh, glad that her timely words had ended their debate.

But the more Judy thought about her daughter's wisdom, the more excited she grew. *Why not?* Carefully, the young mother formed a plan and shared it with her husband. Together they made a commitment.

A few days later, they cleaned out their storeroom and sold several items at a carport sale. Combined with an unexpected check in the mail, the amount equaled their church mission offering pledge.

That Christmas the couple shared only token gifts with each other. As they laid their gift to Jesus under the tree — the money for their mission offering — they discovered a greater joy than the exchange of expensive gifts.

That night the multicolored lights on the tree seemed to dance with joy, almost as if reflecting the twinkle in their little preschooler's eyes. As the family nestled together in their small living room, reading the familiar Christmas story took on a greater meaning. A little child had led them to the foot of the manger where they saw Jesus — the true Light of the World — with new eyes.[35]

Night of Miracles

Then the Lord opened the donkey's mouth.
NUMBERS 22:28

Like a silhouette in the night, the young couple plodded through the streets of Bethlehem. Every place they stopped, they heard the same message: "No room." Tired and discouraged, they bowed weary heads at the last inn. As they turned to go, the innkeeper shouted, "Wait! Come back! I do have a stable. It's not much, but the straw will make a soft bed for your wife."

Donkeys brayed. Cows mooed as if to protest this intrusion. Sheep bleated their objections. The wind outside howled angrily through the trees. But the couple settled in, speaking softly to the animals. The young woman's time to give birth grew near. The animals grew quiet, as if furry mothers were empathizing with this painful act.

Suddenly, a loud wail pierced the night air. Then silence. Deafening silence. Every animal in the stable turned and looked at the young couple—as if listening for the grand finale. And then it came. The sweet cry of a newborn Baby and a mother's hush. "His name is Jesus," whispered the father, as if announcing to his animal congregation.

And then legend says a strange thing happened. One by one, every cow, every sheep, every donkey, every four-footed creature present that wintry night dropped to their knees, as if bowing in humble reverence before the Holy Child. Trees and plants outside began to sway in perfect rhythm, and all of God's creation joined the angels in singing heavenly praise to the Christ born at Bethlehem.

A far-fetched legend? Perhaps. But if God could silence Zechariah, the father of Jesus' forerunner, and make Baalam's donkey speak to reprimand his master, could He not also give voices to His creatures on that wondrous night?

One thing's for sure. When you embrace the miracle of Christ's birth, it's impossible to keep silent.

Following the Star

When they saw the star, they were overjoyed.
MATTHEW 2:10

Carol drove the two boys home from church, they chattered on and on about the lesson they had learned in Sunday school, but Carol couldn't concentrate on what they were saying. She had been struggling to find a job to help meet their family's financial needs. Yet every lead she followed turned out to be a dead end. However, as she waited at a stoplight, something made her listen more closely to the boys' excited chattering.

"These kings saw this star a long way off, and they came prepared with their gifts, and they followed it a long way before they ever got to the Baby," six-year-old Rich said excitedly.

"They took their camels into the desert," three-year-old Robby declared.

"And those kings did all of that, but the Bible says they never got happy until they got to the place where

Baby Jesus was," Rich continued. "They kept on going until they got to the Baby. They followed the star and found joy. Isn't that great, Mom?"

"Yeah, they followed the star to joy," Robby echoed. "Isn't *that* great, Mom?"

Carol thought about the story of the kings. They might have felt that they were following a dead end when they traveled through miles of desert. But they kept going and kept trusting and eventually had something to be happy about.

As they turned into the driveway, Carol began to smile. Maybe her job search wasn't just a series of dead ends after all. Maybe she was really following a star to joy. "Come on, boys," she grinned. "Last one to the house is a king's camel!"

Extravagant Love

*Now to him who is able to do immeasurably
more than all we ask or imagine according to his
power that is at work within us.*
EPHESIANS 3:20

Here's some money for each of you. Combined with your savings, that should be more than enough for your Christmas gifts. Remember, spend your dollars wisely. It's all you have."

Debra gave her daughters final instructions about shopping, and then watched her sister escort them through the mall. They would meet her back at the entrance to the department store in an hour. Debra then set out on her own Christmas shopping hunt.

"Hmm," she said thoughtfully, approaching the perfume counter. "Sweet fragrance for Grandma."

She bought a light floral scent, then headed toward the men's department. "And Grandpa *always* wants a new flannel shirt. This blue plaid will bring out the twinkle in his eyes."

Debra purchased two or three other gifts, then looked at her watch. It was already time to meet her sister and daughters.

Approaching the front of the store, she heard the girls chattering with excitement—both talking at the same time. "Wait 'til you see what we bought!"

"And how much money do you have left?" asked Debra. Both red-faced girls looked down at the floor as they turned their empty pockets inside out.

Debra started to lecture her daughters for spending too much, until a glance from her sister stopped her. Suddenly she realized what the girls had done. They had emptied their pockets for the ones they loved.

Extravagance empties its emotional, physical, and spiritual pockets to lavish love on another in a way that brings pleasure both to the giver and the receiver.[36]

At Christmas, God "emptied His pockets" and gave us the most lavish gift He owned—Jesus.

———————————

Misplaced Expectations

Give thanks in all circumstances,
for this is God's will for you in Christ Jesus.
1 THESSALONIANS 5:18

Most of us at some time indulge in the endless chase for perfection at Christmas: perfect tree, just-right gifts, peaceful gatherings of relatives and friends, no conflicts. And most of us discover quickly the futility of such expectations.

Every year *Dear Abby* prints a familiar story written by Emily Kingsley called, "Welcome to Holland." Emily, a writer, lecturer, and talented mother of an adult child with Down's syndrome, knows about expectations. Others have asked her what it's like raising a child with disabilities. In her story, Emily uses a metaphor. She compares the expectation of a child's birth to planning a vacation trip to Italy. She mentions the joy of deciding on tourist spots to visit, and the anticipation of all the sights you would see upon your arrival.

She then describes the scenario upon landing in your vacation spot. Surely a mistake has been made, because the stewardess on your plane welcomes you not to Italy, but to Holland. You argue, but nothing changes. You are in Holland, and there you will stay.

Anyone who has ever been to Holland knows that tulips, windmills, and Rembrandts make Holland a beautiful place as well. Emily points out that it's just not what you expected. You *planned* on going to Italy.

In her poignant illustration, Kinsgley challenges the reader to focus not on unmet expectations (Italy), but on the beauty of where you are (Holland).

When life doesn't turn out perfectly — the way we planned — *we* have a choice. Whether it's as minor as a holiday gone awry or as major as a Prince Charming that turned into an ugly frog, God wants us to celebrate that "very special, very lovely thing" about our circumstance.

Keep looking. You'll find it.

———————————

The Good of Christmas

How good and how pleasant it is for brethren to
dwell together in unity!
P S A L M   1 3 3 : 1   K J V

In the opening scene of Dickens' *A Christmas Carol*, Scrooge engages in a conversation with his nephew that centers on the good of Christmas. Scrooge is a cantankerous old miser who is at war with the world and wants no one to be joyful or happy; he especially hates holidays. Following an exchange about the celebrating of Christmas, Scrooge tells his nephew that Christmas has never done the nephew any good.

In response the nephew says:

But I am sure I have always thought of Christmastime . . . as a good time: a kind, forgiving, charitable, pleasant time: the only time I know of, in the long calendar of the year, when men and women

194

seem by one consent to open their shut-up hearts freely, and to think of people below them as if they really were fellow-passengers to the grave, and not another race of creatures bound on other journeys. And therefore, uncle, though it has never put a scrap of gold or silver in my pocket, I believe that it has done me good, and will do me good; and I say, God bless it!

What a description of Christmas as it should be! And it's true. Christmas is a time when men and women open their shut-up hearts freely.

Haven't you experienced the joy of a smile from a stranger in response to a hearty "Merry Christmas!"? Remember the contentment you feel when hearing the voices of children singing carols? And how about the sense of wonder and excitement visible in the eyes of a small child as she looks upon a living Nativity scene?

Christmas! It is good, and it does us good! May you, too, say, "God bless it!"

Black-eyed Peas

Sing unto the Lord, O ye saints of his,
and give thanks at the remembrance of his
holiness.
PSALM 30:4 KJV

"Hey, what are you doing?" John asked his wife, Cynthia. It was their first New Year's Eve as husband and wife, and they planned on spending the next day with their families. He was looking forward to watching football games and munching on a variety of "finger foods" throughout the day: vegetable and cheese trays, bite-sized barbecue sausages, Swedish meatballs, celery sticks with cheese filling, and homemade candy.

In stark contrast to his memories, his new bride was sorting black-eyed peas.

"I am preparing the black-eyed peas for tomorrow," Cynthia responded. "It's a tradition; we always eat fresh black-eyed peas on New Year's day."

And with that she promptly dropped a quarter into the pot along with the peas.

"What's with the quarter?" John asked.

"Don't you know anything," she responded. "It is supposed to represent wealth and happiness in the New Year." She then went on to regale him with holiday stories from her childhood.

Family traditions and holidays form an essential foundation for our lives. Each holiday season brings with it a wealth of stories that connect us with our families. For our spiritual life to be its richest, it too must include traditions and celebrations that bring to life the stories of our faith.

Take time this holiday season to share your spiritual memories about your life with Christ with one another. Tell the stories of how Jesus became real for you, and listen to the stories of your loved ones as they share the same.

Good News

Good news from far away
is like cold water to the thirsty.
P R O V E R B S   2 5 : 2 5   T L B

Christmas letters. They come every December if the author is well prepared. Some don't arrive until late January. Those come from the harried and hurried whose lives were just too complicated in late fall to do anything different. But whenever they arrive, they are welcome.

They may be tucked into a greeting card or accompanied by a snapshot. They may come all alone, in their own envelope, bearing their own cancelled stamp. They may be handwritten, computer processed, or churned out by a copying machine. But however they are delivered, they are treasured.

Some fill only one sheet; others ramble on for pages. Some are candid and humorous; others bring concerns and sadness. But all are filled with a common element. All bring news from far away.

Christmas letters. We've all come to expect them each year. That letter may be the only opportunity we have to reconnect with acquaintances and catch up on their family's happenings.

But Christmas letters can be more than newsletters about friends' activities. One woman takes the Christmas letters she receives and divides them into four piles, setting one pile aside for each quarter of the year. During that three-month period she prays for the authors of those letters and, as time permits, even pens a quick note to say "hello." In this way, the Christmas letters she receives each year bring her good news but also bring the sender her thoughts and prayers. Her simple gesture creates a refreshing circle of love.

What will you do with your Christmas letters this year?

———————————

References

Unless otherwise indicated, all Scripture quotations are taken from the *Holy Bible, New International Version®*, niv®. Copyright © 1973, 1978, 1984 by the International Bible Society. Used by permission of Zondervan Publishing House. All rights reserved.

Scripture quotations marked kjv are taken from the *King James Version* of the Bible.

Scripture quotations marked nasb are taken from the *New American Standard Bible*. Copyright © The Lockman Foundation 1960, 1962, 1963, 1968, 1971, 1972, 1973, 1975, 1977. Used by permission.

Scripture quotations marked ncv are taken from *The Holy Bible, New Century Version,* copyright © 1987, 1988, 1991 by Word Publishing, Dallas, Texas 75039. Used by permission.

Scripture quotations marked nkjv are taken from *The New King James* Version. Copyright © 1979, 1980, 1982, 1994, by Thomas Nelson, Inc.

Verses marked tlb are taken from *The Living Bible,* copyright © 1971. Used by permission of Tyndale House Publishers, Inc., Wheaton, Illinois 60189. All rights reserved.

Scripture quotations marked the message are taken from the message. Copyright © by Eugene H. Peterson, 1993, 1994, 1995, 1996. Used by permission of NavPress Publishing Group.

Endnotes

---

1. (pp. 10, 11) Thomas J. Bums, "The Second Greatest Christmas Story Ever," *Reader's Digest* (December 1989).

2. (pp. 22, 23) Author of story unknown.

3. (pp. 24, 25) Dale E. Galloway, *You Can Win with Love* (Irvine: Harvest House, 1976).

4 (pp. 42, 43) Steven Ger, "The Undying Flame," *Kindred Spirit* (Winter 1999).

5. (pp. 72, 73) *Dallas Morning News* (February 2, 1992).

6. (p. 81) *The Christmas Card Songbook* (Milwaukee: Hal Leonard Publishing, 1991).

7. (pp. 82, 83) Dale E. Galloway, *You Can Win with Love* (Irvine: Harvest House, 1976).

8. (pp. 86, 87) Leslie Flynn, *Come Alive with Illustrations* (Grand Rapids: Baker Book House, 1988).

9. (p. 87) Rebecca Barlow Jordan © 2000.

10. (p. 97) Craig McDonald, *Greenville Herald Banner* (December 26, 1997).

11. (p. 99) Gerald Bath, "Long Walk Included," http://www.sermons.org/Christmasillustrations l-1999.html#4.

12. (pp. 104, 105) Lois Kaufman, compiler, *Christmas: A Time for Family* (White Plains: Peter Pauper Press, 1998).

13. (pp. 108, 109) Rev. Douglas Showalter, "Nowhere Else to Go," www.heartwarmers.com, 21 December 1999,

http://dispatch.mail- list.com/archives/heartwarmers/ msg00490.html.

14. (pp. 112, 113) Mack McDonald, "Gift Ideas," *The Dallas Morning News* (December 12, 1992).

15. (pp. 118, 119) *The Christmas Card Songbook* (Milwaukee: Hal Leonard Publishing, 1991).

16. (pp. 126, 127) Dr. Norman Vincent Peale, *Creative Help for Daily Living* (Pawling: Foundation for Christian Living, December 1970).

17. (p. 129) Joe L. Wheeler, *Christmas in My Heart, Book 2* (Hagerstown: Review and Herald Publishing Association, 1993).

18. (p. 131) Marv Knox, "Twice Blessed," *Baptist Standard* (February 23, 2000).

19. (pp. 136, 137) *Dallas Morning News* (December 25, 1992).

20. (pp. 138, 139) Gary Rummier, "Girl, 8, Lets Down Her Hair for Wig Charity," *Wichita Falls Times Record News* (February 26, 2000).

21. (pp. 142, 143) Leslie Flynn, *Come Alive with Illustrations* (Grand Rapids: Baker Book House, 1988).

22. (pp. 146, 147) Ibid.

23. (pp.150, 151) Niki Anderson, "Straw in the Crib," *Home Life* (December 1994).

24 (p. 155) Rebecca Barlow Jordan, "What Gift Have I For Jesus?" *Day Spring Cards.*

25. (pp. 156, 157) Dale E. Galloway, You *Can Win with Love* (Irvine: Harvest House, 1976).

26. (p. 157) Lawrence Pearsall Jacks, Frank S. Mead, ed., *The Encyclopedia of Religious Quotations* (Westwood: Fleming H. Revell, 1965).

27. (pp. 160, 161) Ruth Bell Graham, It's *My Turn* (Old Tappan: Fleming H. Revell).

28. (pp. 162, 163) Robert Fulghum, *All I Really Need to Know 1 Learned in Kindergarten* (New York: Ballantine Books).

29. (pp. 164, 165) *The Christmas Card Songbook* (Milwaukee: Hal Leonard Publishing, 1991).

30. (p. 167) Sue Monk Kidd, *When the Heart Waits* (New York: HarperSanFrancisco, 1990).

31. (pp. 168, 169) Reagan Graham, "Special Needs Class Brings JOY to Tomball, *Baptist Standard* (March 1, 2000).

32. (pp. 176, 177) Allen G. Breed, "Fulfilling a Final Prescription," *Greenville Herald Banner* (May 7, 1999).

33. (pp. 178, 179) Dr. Norman Vincent Peale, *Creative Help for Daily Living,* (Pawling: Foundation for Christian Living, December 1970).

34 (pp. 182, 183) Dennis Rainey, *Moments Together for Couples* (Ventura: Regal Publishing, 1995).

35. (pp. 184, 185) Rebecca Barlow Jordan, adapted from "The Quiet Place," *Chandler Arizonan* (1980).

36. (pp. 190, 191) Larry and Rebecca Jordan, *Marriage Toners,* Weekly Exercises to Strengthen Your Relationship (Grand Rapids: FlemingJ. Revell, 1995).

Additional copies of this book and other titles the "Quiet Moments with God" devotional series are available from
your local bookstore:

Breakfast with God
Coffee Break with God
Sunset with God
Tea Time with God
Daybreak with God
Through the Night with God
In the Garden with God
In the Kitchen with God